FENG

FENG
The Other Canary Story

Written by

DAVID WILKES

Feng

Copyright © 2024 by David Wilkes. All rights reserved.

No part of this publication may be reproduced, stored in a retrieval system or transmitted in any way by any means, electronic, mechanical, photocopy, recording or otherwise without the prior permission of the author except as provided by USA copyright law.

The opinions expressed by the author are not necessarily those of URLink Print and Media.

1603 Capitol Ave., Suite 310 Cheyenne, Wyoming USA 82001
1-888-980-6523 | admin@urlinkpublishing.com

URLink Print and Media is committed to excellence in the publishing industry.

Book design copyright © 2024 by URLink Print and Media. All rights reserved.

Published in the United States of America

Library of Congress Control Number: 2024910147
ISBN 978-1-68486-778-3 (Paperback)
ISBN 978-1-68486-788-2 (Hardback)
ISBN 978-1-68486-781-3 (Digital)

07.05.24

Chapter 1

In the fall of 1989, there lived a couple in an apartment in the suburbs of New Haven, CT. And their names were Gabriel and Rachel, who were in a two-year rocky relationship. Rachel Winters worked as a part time waitress and had become pregnant. And she was questioning their status, to better understand their future. And she wanted no drama, regarding how his family felt about her. Only, this time around bringing a child into this world without a father. Gabriel Lord at the age of 22, wasn't ready to commit to a future with her. And he was a smart, determined person with a presents about himself. And he was in the US army as an enlisted soldier, and had gotten called in for active duty. And they agreed to break up, but stayed in contact, even after the birth of their son. And their son was born in the spring of 1990, and she named him Feng. Gabriel had missed the birth of his son due to his duty. However, an hour later, by video chat, he seen his son. And the nurse had held the phone, while she spoke resting with their son. And she had gotten the name from a friend named Polly Feng. And they had known each other for a good two years, becoming close friends. Polly was a Christian woman she met at a church called, Army of Elohim. And the church was in New Haven, CT.

Rachel, three months later, had received bad news from a Causalty assistance officer at her new apartment. And he said that Gabriel had gotten kill in the line of duty, and felt sorry for her. And he hugged her, as she began to break down and cry. And she was 19 years old with a three-month-old son. And she, not being ready for motherhood, didn't know who to turn to. Rachel's family had turned their back on her, disagreeing with the relationship. So, she after a few days, was in a very dark place in her life. And she wanted Gabriel back, but knew because of his death, it would never be. So, she at the time was dealing with depression, anxiety and the pressure of being a single parent. And she now giving it some thought, had reached out to the Feng's by phone, and was invited to their house a few days later. So, that day, she spoke with Polly about her neglected situation. And she revealed her plans, and it became frowned upon. Polly disappointed accompany by her husband had asked, "I understand people or family members... But, why would you neglect your own son?" She then frowns at the comment answering, "I love my son, Polly !... I just wasn't ready to become a mother."

So, the Feng family had agreed to adopt him into their family. And they lived in the East Haven area, and had kept his last name. Polly was barren without children, and wanted a family. So, she and her husband, Paster Lo Feng counted him a blessing. Now, Rachel, knowing he was in good hands, quit her job days later. And she packed up and left the state, to start her life all over again. And they legally began raising him as their own son, teaching him and others the bible at home. And she would sing, and hold him everywhere she went.

Lo later had gain four saved friends, by teaching bible study at church. And the young men became beacons, and their names were Shepard, Tommy, James and Bushiri. And these men soon became part of Lo's ministries. And they left the church with bishop Meyers blessing. And the deacons later worked with him in and out of state. And were introduced to his son, Feng .

Feng very young, had accepted Jesus at the age of 6. And his parents would invite him into their praying room to pray together. And the presents of the lord would fill the room. And they would witness angels with and without wings appearing to them. And the angels gave their names, revelations, and would sing. And they also understood time, the environment, situations, relationships and character. And they kept a chart of the angel names, and below it was written Psalm 32:8. And their names being Lamuel, Uriel, Phanuel, Kuriel, Adriel, Dream, Rashael, Eloniel, Sonamael, Anakiel, Eliel, Sarliquin, Sara bell, Saal, Cami el, Rubiel, Thurubibel, Gegudiel and many more. And the angels that manifested were beautiful to look upon. Serious looking, and giant-sized explaining that they're not of the world. And this help build his faith in knowing they service a mighty God. And his father would draw the angels, to identify the types made known to them. And the Feng's supported him in all activities, giving him a great childhood. And he around this time, had learned self-defend by his uncle named Ken, for a short period of time.

And he grew to be an Intelligent, strong and humble person. And he was grateful for being adopted but always felt he wasn't. And he grew to be nearly six feet tall, well built and bald with a beard. And his mother hasn't been a part of his life, even til this day. He later stops going to church, given no reason why.

Feng grew up with his childhood friend named Angel, in the neighborhood. And he was a good friend, with a lust for women. And he always looked out for Feng, and later became a bouncer. And he knew Feng needed a job, so he introduced him one night to the owner named Greg Rendeci. And the owner was a down to earth, no-nonsense kind of guy. And the club was named Jades, on Conway Ave in downtown New Haven. Feng had gotten hired in November of 2015.

And in that present month and year, one night at the club. There was an event called, Hip hop Night. And the owner had called for a meeting with the bouncers in his office upstairs. Ten minutes later, they stood before him in gossip. And he had eleven bouncers, and their names were Brain, Tom Tom, Tylor, Angel, Feng, Jason, Lewis, Nicki, Michael, Chris and Columbus. Greg, about to start the meeting, had noticed Feng was absent. And he becoming curious asked," Where is Feng?" And the other bouncers didn't know where he was. Greg replied, "Somebody go, and tell him I need him." Angel then volunteered to go find him. And he left the office, heading downstairs to the main hall to begin the search.

Feng at the time, was outside the club taking a break close to the alley. And people were passing him on a cool night. And his mind was on making career moves, and moving out of his parents' house. Then came a long dark hair, beautiful young lady catching his eye named, Nia Yung. And she was coming from the parking lot, with two of her friends named Brenda and Katie. And she was wearing a black halter top with blue jeans, crossing the street with a purse conversating. And he kept staring at her, admiring her beauty. Then Angel came outside from the entrance, and saw him. And he met with Feng shouted," FENG !... THE BOSS WANTS TO SEE YOU !" The ladies walking had seen Feng, and got her attention. And she saw him and laughed, making her way inside with them. And he looks at Angel asking, "Did you see that girl in that black halter top, brah ?" Angel answers," Yeah!... Why are you outside anyways?" Feng replied," I needed a break man." They then made their way back, and headed to the office.

Greg at the time, was talking about the bouncers not doing their job right. And they came inside the office with all eyes on them. Greg, now crossing his arms, had watched Feng close the door shut. And he in a sarcastic manner says," Feng, so nice of you to join us!" A few of the bouncers had chucked at the comment. Greg saw and says," Listen up, if any of you don't want to be here... Shake my hand and leave!" And he, now in a demanding voice, continues to say, "This is a business! This is the highest paid club in town... Instead of complaining to me about long hours, you should be stopping underage girls from coming inside my club!... Don't ever let me catch any of you doing this again!... Are we clear?" The bouncers all in agreeance answered," Yes sir!"

Greg then dismissed all the bouncers but told Brian to stay behind. Brain was his right-hand man, and he needed to speak with him privately. Feng and Angel were making their way downstairs into the main hall. And he glanced at Angel asking, "Who would let underage girls inside a club?" He answers, "I have no clue... It's hard to say, Brian allowed it." Nia at the time, not watching where she was going, bumps into Feng. And she immediately apologizes to him saying "Sorry! Sorry!" And he recognizing it was her, smile and answered, "It's alright." And she now remembering his face from outside, had awkwardly asked, "You work here?" Feng standing across from Angel answers," Yes, I do. Why?" She smiling, reply,.... I didn't think you were a jerk or anything." Feng began to laugh at her and asked ,"Can we talk?" Angel then got his attention by waving shouted," FIGHT NEAR THE STAGE!"

Now, there was a fight between two men close to the stage where the DJ was. Nia's friend Brenda came and tapped her from behind asking, "Where were you?" She begins to follow her back to their seat and gave no answer. Feng with Angel made their way over as the people moved aside. Angel then stops one guy named," Tylor" from punching the other. Feng held the other guy named," Lloyd "from behind asking, "Why are you two fighting?"

Before Tylor could answer, Brain had rushed over to them saying, "Greg said to kick them out!" And they immediately did what they were told.

Feng shortly after that issue had looked around for Nia, but doesn't see her. And he asks around the club, but nobody knows who, or where she was. He then stood and gave up. And he from behind, heard her voice asked," Talk about what?" Feng then turned around and saw her. And she was walking towards him smiling with her friends. And she met with him asked," What is your name?" Feng smiling answered, "Feng Winters!" Katie looked at him says," He's cute, Nia!" She now became curious, begins to cross her arms about his name asked, "Feng, is your name?" He answered, "I'm not Asian, but yeah!" Angel then walked over to him, and said that Greg was coming. Nia said, "Take down my number, Feng." And he immediately hurries up, and uses his phone from the back pocket to get her number. Angel then smiled, watching them get along.

Brain with Greg were outside watching the two men they kicked out. And threats were issued out between them. And two bouncers had come outside, to make sure nothing happens. Greg frustrated with the situation, says, "What's the problem guys! I have a business to run!" Lloyd answered, "He thinks me, and his girlfriend are more than friends!" The People around the club were watching. Greg arguably asked, "He thinks?... Listen!... If this happens again, I will call the cops!... Now, get out of here!... Both of you!" Tylor's girlfriend named Anne had come out of the club. And she seen him in a worried manner asks, "Where were you?... And why are you outside?" Tylor watching her approach him says, "Why is your friend Lloyd here?... You told me you were at your girlfriend's house... You lied to me!" The couple began to argue and walk away. Greg then told the door man to watch them. And he and the fellas had gone back inside. Lloyd, being irritated, had walked away. And his personality, could be blunt at times, and he was indeed a lady's man.

He then receives a call near his car, from a friend named Jason Hill. And his friend's character, was a by the book kind of guy. And he saw, and answered it asking, "Hey Jason, can I call you back?" Jason immediately says, "Lloyd, listen!... I have an opportunity for you to work with me, bro! You looked out for me, now it's my turn... Officer Malone, Chance and detective Ronald saw something in me... Of course, you don't know these men, but... They saw me wrestle with a man threatening to kill his ex-girlfriend outside a restaurant. And after they arrested him, they spoke with me about becoming a cop, and I was down." Lloyd wondering what's his angle stood, and opened the car door says, "So, they talked you into becoming a cop?... What opportunity are you talking about?... You know I'm a realtor going through a tough time right now. You don't owe me anything, were friends." Hill reply back," Becoming a cop, like me... I know were friends, you said you're going through a tough time, right?... When we last spoke, you said the same exacted thing months back." Lloyd thought on it, now seated, resting his head on the headrest answers, "Like, seven months ago... But, I don't know... Let me think about it, ok... I had no idea you became a cop... How long have you been a cop?" Hill answers, "About ten months now, you're the first outside my family to know... And it wasn't easy Chase... Don't you think on it too long !... I already told my Lieutenant about you, and were hoping to see you with us." Lloyd continues to think on it turning the engine on says, "Take care, Hill!" Hill answered, "Alright!" Lloyd then hung-up, and threw the phone at the passenger seat driving home. And he later, walked around the living room with a made-up mind to join the force. And he called Hill regarding the police academy. And after talking for an hour, Hill mentioned that he will be in touch within a few days. Lloyd had thanked him before hanging up, and relaxed on the living room couch.

The next day on a windy Sunday morning at the Feng residents. Feng was in bed and became awoken, hearing trash cans being thrown around. And he heard his mother's voice shouting," STOP IT!... STOP IT!" Feng worried, had left the room in a Tink top with pajamas pants. And he raced downstairs, unsure of what awaits him, to the front yard and saw nothing. Polly was in the back yard trying to calm Lo down. And she begged him to stop by holding his right arm. And he kept shaking his hand, away from her out of anger. And their neighbors had come to see what was going on. Feng then met with them in the backyard. Polly saw and called him over to help calm Lo down. And he looks at the two trash cans halfway full. And he saw garbage all around them, and in a worried manner asks," What happened?... Dad? Mom?" Polly worried about her husband answers, "Your father wasn't feeling well... So, we went to see a doctor this morning... And the doctor told him that he has Lung cancer!... It's from all that smoking before I met your father and after." Lo with a load voice in rage shouted, "I DON'T DESERVE THIS ! I HAVENT SMOKE IN SIXTEEN YEARS!" Polly begins to shed tears letting his arm go. And she wipes her tears worried and slowly asked," Can we count on you to stay healthy?" Lo calming down, had looks at everyone feeling ashamed said," Of course you can ."Polly then comforts Lo with a hug. And their neighbors, hearing the situation, had gone back inside their homes. And their son immediately started picking up the garbage, worried about his father's condition.

Feng later went back to the room for his phone, regarding messages at the computer desk. And he saw a miss call from Nia, and a message left to voice mail. And he heard the message on her questioning where to go. Feng then excitedly called her back, and she answered hello? He asked," Nia, it's Feng... Where you wanna go?" She given it some thought answers, "The West haven beach... Is that alright?" Feng answers, "Yeah!... What time?" Nia hearing the excitement in his voice asked, "Will six works?" He answered, "Yes!... Yes, six works. "Nia then chuckled and says, "14 Melly Street... It's in New Haven... See you at six!" Feng thought on the comment made as he hung up. And he checked his alarm clock at the computer desk, and saw it was only 11:47 a.m. Feng was indeed happy and couldn't wait for the date.

Feng then heard his mother loudly talking in the kitchen, so he went to go tell her. And when he entered the kitchen, he saw her alone washing dishes. And he curiously asked, "Mom, who were you talking to?" Polly worrying about Lo answers, "You father... Why?" Feng in concern about where his father went asked," Where did he go?" Polly now finishing the last dish answers ," He just left, I don't know... Let him cool down." And she turned the sink off, and reached for a paper towel near to dry her hands. And after drying them, she threw the towel into the trash can and met with him, asking,"Did you want to tell me or your father about something?" Feng feeling it wasn't the right time said," No." He then thought about his father's smoking habit asked," Mom?... Dad's smoking habit back then... Was it a lot?" Polly then took a breather and answers," Yes, before and after knowing him... Your father and I met at a club back then... And I was dancing while he was smoking... And I had noticed something different about this guy, like a light on him... He was a backslider at the time... Lo and I got to know each other after a few dates. And he had mentioned a church he used to go to... We up and decided to visit the old church one day... And you know that old saying, that the rest was history." Feng surprised begin to cross his arms asking," Dancer?" She nodded yes and answers," Exotic dancer... I was lost, but now I am found, son... I now dance to praise and worship music. And the lord would begin to show me things when I would dance... Maybe it was time I told you that story. Glad were saved, hun... Tell you something funny... When your father would feel the spirit hit him in church, he would skip around... That was so funny." Feng then heard her laugh, but was now in thought of his father's health.

Nia at that same hour, was home with her brother named, Alex. Now Alex, her older brother, was very selfish and to himself. And she had been living with him for quite some time now. And she was upstairs in her room, in the closet for the date. And she heard her brother's voice outside talking with a man. She then went to the window and saw him in the front yard talking with their cousin named, Steve Liang. And she began to open the window to eavesdrop on their conversation.

Alex says, "I've been working long hours at work!... Nia was talking about living with Aunt Lilliana in New Jersey again... But these past few weeks, she had a change of heart... I don't know..." Steve with his arms crossed says, "You should come and work for me... You've already told me your boss doesn't like you." Alex, becoming curious, asked," Doing what?... I know Aunt Maggie was going to leave you the wine store, but... never mind." Steve says, "Whatever you're making, I'll double it!" Alex feeling pressured, quickly replies," I can't." Steve then walks up to him asking, "Why?... Family takes care of family, right?" Alex, avoiding an argument, looked away. Ad he becomes nerved, with his hands in his pocket answers," I can't, but thanks." There immediately, was an awkward pause between them. Steve, reading his body language, knowing that he knew something, begins to laugh. And he again says, "Family takes care of family... You remember that, Yung!" Steve then left. And she moved away from the window being bothered. Alex then came inside the house into the living room with the TV on. And she was coming downstairs to meet with him, having questions. And she met with him asking, "What did he want?" Alex immediately knew from the comment, that she heard them talk. And he ignored the question, wanting to watch TV. And she immediately took notice of him ignoring her. And she became irritated, given an attitude says," I'm not 10 years old, you know!" He heard but continued to watch TV. She then grabs the remote from the couch and turns the TV off. And he got upset with her and shouts," WOULD YOU STOP IT ALREADY!... GOSH, NOT EVERYTHING IS ABOUT YOU!" Alex then walks away from her out of anger and left the house. And she saw him drive off, and was left wondering .

One hour later behind a wine store on 23 Howard Ave. Steve was in conversation with nine guys around their sport cars. And his character was a mild manner strategist with muscle. Those that knew him, feared him because of his mild manner. And he having their attention says, "My idea for this city is to remain lord of the crime... Shawn tried to keep peace around here and was murdered. We bring fear back into the people, nothing moves without me knowing... Let it be known." The men were all in agreeance nodding their heads. And he gave the crew orders to carry out.

Feng that afternoon, had arrived on time, at the Yung residents in a black sports car. Nia at the time, was waiting for him on the porch casually dressed. And she saw a car parked in front and wondered who it was. And he got out and waved at her. She now came excitedly, and met with him. And he opens and closes her door, watching her smile. And she reached for the seatbelt saying," Thank you." Feng then glanced at the house, about to sit and closed his door said, "Nice house!" And she answered, "It's my brother's house." And they took off, and within 15 minutes had arrived at the West Haven beach, with very few people there.

And after being parked, they got out looking at each other smiling. And after locking the car, they begin to walk and view everything. And she glanced at him saying, "I come here a lot... Being in the office all day is boring, thank God for Brenda my coworker... Yeah, she gets me going." Feng was looking at the ocean view, listening to her nodding. And she glanced at a couple about to pass by, and out of curiosity, says," So, tell me about yourself... Are you always this quite." He asked, "What you want to know about me?" She then began to hold her hands up, and in a sarcastic manner replies, "We can start with your name." Feng laughs and answers," My mother was friends with a Christian family. And their last name is Feng.... And that's my family." Nia reviewing what was said asked, "Your first name is Feng?"

They then stopped walking as he answers," Yes... Feng Winters is my full name... I'm their only son." And she in remembrance, of the last name says, "There is a man, that preaches all around the New Haven area with four deacons known as Paster Lo Feng." Feng then laughs at the mentioning of his father's name. And she, becoming curious of his laughter asked, "Why are you laughing!... I don't get it, wait a minute?..... Is he your father?" Feng smiles and answered, "Yes he is." And she was amazed and didn't know what else to say. Feng now having questions for her had asked, "What did you do this morning?... What do you like to eat?... I wanna know more about you." She then smiled, and kissed him on the cheek, leaving him stunned. And they continued to walk again. Nia feeling comfortable with him, answers," You've already made my day!... I was home relaxing... I like mostly everything except spicy and fatty foods... I really can't do spicy... I'll be waving my hand at you for water." Feng then laughs at the remark. And she not getting his sense humor asked, "What's funny?... You said you wanted to know more about me, right?" He then gazed at her for a second answering," You crack me up in a cute way." They then joined hands, laughing at the comment. And they continued talking that afternoon about everything. And he later had brough her back home. And a week later, he had introduced her to his mother. And she had met Lo, days before, due to Feng's absence at home. Polly and Nia then developed a bond and had exchange numbers.

During that time, Lo wanted to do a few revival services outside downtown New Haven. And he did a commercial, and the services were posted all over town. And when the revival had started, many people came out.

Alex from time to time would drive by, and see the Feng's. And he would see the deacons near Lo in service. And he would hear about them, but would never socialize with them.

Feng two weeks after the revival, on a chilly afternoon outside the house had gotten a text message from his uncle Ken. And he texted, "Feng get your butt over here, and learn how to kick again." He laughed at the text reaching for his keys with a mind to go visit. And he unlocked his car parked in the opened garage. And he closed the garage by a switch near, driving off to meet Ken.

12 minutes later, he arrived at Ken's house. And he parked behind his red sport car. And he gets out of the car hearing Ken's voice striking something hard in the back yard. He then came to the back yard, viewing this huge 3,487 square foot home, to meet with Ken. And he had a bamboo build in tent in the backyard, for his martial arts training. Ken inside the tent was kicking a kickboxing bag, harder and harder. Feng entering in the tent, from behind asked," You're still doing the kicking thing?" Ken then stopped and faced him answered," Still?... I never stopped, Feng. You stop coming over was what had happened... I called you over to see if you still got it." Feng laughed and answered," I was fourteen then. "Ken frowned at the comment and said," I don't understand. You learned how to defend yourself, right?... Uses it or lose it, Feng." Feng then stood to the bag, taking a breather and

started to kick. And after a few minutes had gone by, Ken says," Feng, you know... I have one daughter, that's a kick boxing champ under my studio. But, no son... My brother on the other hand has a son. That would be you, Feng... And when you were fourteen, I thought you would've been my son also. "Feng then stopped and shouts ," I STOPPED BECAUSE YOU WERE BEING TOO HARD ON ME!... MY FATHER STOPPED YOU!... DO YOU REMEMBER?" He nodded yes and answers," I do... Feng, this is my way of spending time with you, then, and now... Without being too hard on you, I apologize." Feng now feeling surprised and awkward says," It took you this long to say I'm sorry?" He nodded yes, and in a sarcastic manner says," I'm not saved, Feng... I was a very prideful person then, and was blinded by it... And pride nearly cost me my marriage, and I love my family... When I see Lo and Polly together, it gives me hope... If they can change, so can I... My wife too." Feng then understood, watching him go to a chair for a towel. And he, using the towel to wipe the sweat from his neck says," And yes Feng, you are my son too... You want a protein shake?" Feng being caught off guard immediately answered," Sure, what flavor?" Ken smiled and says," Any... After you give it a go again... Now, start kicking!" Feng then focused on the bag again, kicking with Ken's help.

    20 minutes later, they went inside to the kitchen to talk and have a protein shake. And his daughter, named Michelle Feng, was 19 years old and saved. And she was at the kitchen table seated, on her phone. And his wife Susan wasn't home yet. And his wife's character was kind, but could be very nosey at times. And his daughter's character was down to earth, athletic and she had a good sense of humor. And she, being surprised to see Feng, had gotten up and hugged him. Michelle hadn't seen him in over six months and because of this, it gave a heartwarming reconnection to the family.

Two years had now passed, and it became June of 2017. And it was 78 degrees and sunny that afternoon. Lloyd with Hill, at the time were patrolling in the New Haven area. Hill driving around had wanted to stir up a conversation, seeing his partner was bored. So, he looked at Lloyd and says, "See, I told you we would be working together bro... I know you're still the rookie... But, wait til the action starts." Lloyd had smiled at the remark looking away. And he looks at his watch out of boredom, ignoring his partner. Hill knew he was bored says, "You won't be bored for long, bro... We don't know what today will bring, right?... Ever wonder what Jesus is like?... I believe it's in Matthew 10:34, where he said.... Think not that I am come to send peace on earth: I came not to send peace, but a sword... Chase, ain't that something? "Lloyd smirks at the comment already annoyed answers," Listen!... All I want is not to be called rookie or anything, bro. The fellas already told me that you're a little jealous that I became a cop earlier than you... And I don't care what today will bring!... And regarding Jesus, I ain't touching that... So, please, be quite." Hill heard, and regrated suring his feelings with the other officers. And he then changed the subject, with a question in mind regarding the news asked," What are your thoughts regarding the news.... Detective Miller being crooked, and killed by another detective?" Lloyd being in thought answered," I believe they were in a car together... He made it a waste of two years over money. And the news did a good job, not exposing him as a detective... Because it would've made it harder for the next detective." Hill then makes a right turn heading downtown. And they were waiting for the Police station to radio anything, but nothing came.

And they reached a stop light and stopped on red. And the civilians then got the sign to cross. And two men and one woman were crossing over at the time. Hill then glance at Lloyd asking," So, how are things home?" And before he could answer, a guy wearing a hoodie had run and snatches a lady's purse from behind. Hill quickly turned the siren on and got out of the car. And he told Lloyd to stay in the car to follow, and radio it in. And the lady yelled for help, watching Hill chase after the guy on foot. And he saw the guy running left, into traffic yelled, "STOP! I TOLD YOU TO STOP !"

Feng at the time, was seated at an outdoor patio restaurant near the chase, having tacos with water. And he and the customers within seconds, had witnessed the officer yelling at the thug. And his partner had driven past the thug, and stomped on the breaks. And he parked in the middle of the street. And he gets out of the patrol car, with a plan to block him aware of his surroundings. And the thug began to panic seeing the officer in front, and another behind him. And the thug had ran, and stopped at the patio fence, looking for a way out. And he saw a big knife near a plate, with food at a couple's table. And he immediately jumped over the fence, grabbing the knife from the table, looking at Lloyd. And the lady at the table became frightened, and started to scream. Feng then got up from his seat wanting to help. And the thug saw Lloyd jump over the fence, to meet with him. And he threw the purse at Lloyd, aiming the knife now at the heart. And he, within seconds, had thrown the knife at him, catching the purse. Feng was already in motion, tackling Lloyd to the ground. And they heard a car alarm go off. And the thug had jumps over the fence, and makes a run for it. And his partner, quickly pulled out a gun from his holster, taking a clear aim from behind. And he, without hesitation, focused on the leg and fired one shot. And the bullet stopped the thug in the middle of the street. And he ran and met with the thug, face down on the ground in pain bleeding. And he heard the thug scream, holding his leg, begging for mercy. Hill aiming the gun yells, "DON'T MOVE!... YOU HAVE THE RIGHT TO REMAIN SILENT!" And the people at the restaurant, and all over had come to watch. And the thug with one hand, had covered his face in shame. Lloyd gets up from the ground with Feng. And he amazed at the situation reply, "Thank you, sir!" Feng nodded, and begins to walk away says, "The knife is behind you." He then saw the knife stuck to a parked car door, with the alarm still sounding. And he saw the thug being handcuffed. Lloyd then met with them, and loudly asked, "WAS THE KNIFE MEANT TO KILL ME?... HEY!... ANSWER ME!" Hill with the thug had walked to the cop car. And he then glanced at Lloyd asking, "Lloyd, why the attitude?... Where is that guy that save you?" Lloyd looks around, and didn't see Feng, answers, "No clue... All this for a purse." And the owner of the car sounding, had come out of the restaurant complaining. And a few customers, had pointed to the thug for the reason being. And after putting the thug in the cop car, the cops left.

Later in the evening, as it rains very light. Jades club had a House music event, and a great crowd were waiting for the doors to be opened. And the bouncers were all having a meeting in Greg's office again. And the owner looks at all the bouncers with Brain by his side says, "Alright, let's get to it... I have been watching you all for months... And I need a second supervisor or manager... What I am looking for is someone who will be my right-hand man. Well, left because Brain is my right... Someone who can get the job done with class, and with that being said." Greg looks at Feng and said," Feng!..." The bouncers then focused on him, and gave a round of applause. And he smiles and asked," You pick me, Greg?" Greg laughed at the remark, walking over. And he shook his hand, saying, "Yes, you Feng... You're my second manager, and congratulations... Thank you for all your hand work."

Angel then walks over to him saying, "It's about time, man! "Now, Greg in good spirits says, "Non alcoholic drinks on me tonight... But, let's have some class gentlemen... You guys are still on the clock... Alright, now open the doors." Brian watching the bouncers leave, had walked over to congratulated him with a handshake, says, "You moved on up, bro!... You know I am the first manager; Glad it was you." Feng nodded and replied ," Thank, Brain." Angel than says," Come downstairs and celebrate, bro!"

And two bouncers at the time, had opened the door for the people. Feng and Angel had made their way to the bar, ordering club soda. And they told the bartender, the boss said no charge and received their drinks. Angel then raises his cup saying," Cheers, bro!" Feng saw and raised his cup too. And they drank at the same time and went to work. Now, 10 minutes later, the club was pumping with good vibes.

Chapter 2

To the right of the main hall, by the stage was a couple dancing. And there near, was a young man named Robbie Wong, watching the girlfriend in a lustful manner. And he was a member of Steve's crew who loved to rob. Robbie after a few minutes, began to intrude between the two. And the boyfriend shouts," YEAH!... WHAT ARE YOU DOING?" Robbie immediately pulled the girlfriend close, and started touching her hips. And she surprised, by his actions had frowned, and felt uncomfortable had pushed him away, yelled, "HEY!... GET YOUR HANDS OFF OF ME!" And the boyfriend upset now stood to him. And the people dancing around them, had stopped to watch everything. Now, Brian from afar, had seen the two men in a hostile manner. And he making his way, had called another bouncer nearby named Tylor to follow. And the two bouncers approach Robbie and the couple. Robbie being nervous of their size and height, asked, "What's going on? "The lady with her boyfriend pointed at him, saying, "This guy was touching me!" And the boyfriend agreed, nodding. Robbie then faced the people with an attitude says, "I just wanted to show her a good time!" The boyfriend disliking his rude manner reply, "Dude!... She's not your girlfriend !"Brian then focused on Robbie's back being turned says, "You, let's go!" And he immediately grabs and dragged Robbie from behind. Tylor was calming the couple down at the time. And he watched everyone begin to dance to a new song. Robbie, feeling embarrassed, began to reach into his pocket for a short knife. And he grabbed it, and quickly stabbed Brian in the left leg. And the bouncer had shouted out loud in pain, releasing him. And he, in the state of shock, had fallen holding his leg. And he tries to stop the bleeding. Robbie now saw an opportunity to take advantage of his right leg. And he caught Brian off guard, and stabbed the leg. He then ran out of the club. And the people around them saw, and moved away. Tylor saw the crowd move, hearing Brian's voice in pain. And he runs over to him, and became worried asking, "What happen?... Where is Feng?" And he then got down on one knee, and saw the blood. And he also saw a knife in his leg. Tylor looking around for help loudly shouts," FENG!... FENG!" Feng and Angel at the bar heard his voice calling. And they immediately ran over, and met with them. And the DJ removing his headset heard and saw Brian. And he immediately stopped the music out of concern.

Robbie at the time was running to his car down the street. And he, being surprised, had seen Steve talking with two members in a car. And he saw that they were across from his car yelled ,"STEVE!" And they all heard, and saw him run to meet with them. Steve, frowning about the unknown had asked, "Why are you running ?"Robbie then met up with them. And he catches his breath answers," I almost kill a bouncer in Jades!... Why are you out here boss?" Steve then looked at the club from a distance asking, "Did he make trouble for you?" Robbie taken another breather answers, "Yes, he did... And I think they called the cops." They now saw two of their beautiful women, come out a yogurt store. And they had crossed the street, and met with them to gossip. Steve now asked Robbie for his key, and received it. And he told the fellas he'd spoken with, to hide Robbie til things had calmed down. Robbie had gotten in their car, and they left. Steve threw the key to one of the girls. And he then took notice, that the people around were watching, yelled, "LET'S MOVE!" One lady rushed into the car with him and left. And the other woman drove Robbie's car to follow them.

The people at the time, were told to leave the club due to the affair. And the owner inside the club, was asking Brian question about the guy. Greg asked," Do you know what this guy looks like? I already called 911, the ambulance is on its way." Brain answers, "Of course I know what he looks like. He is Asian, five foot three with no facial hair… His fingerprints are all on the knife." Brain was seated and being helped by a bartender named Linda. And she provided him with towels for the bleeding. Feng and the other bouncers were around him for comfort. Angel looking at the blood on the towels, sarcastically said, "Where is a cop when you need one!" The bouncers found it funny and laughed at the comment made.

Officer Hill and Lloyd then arrived inside the entrance of the club. Hill saw and met with everyone at the bar asking," Is Greg the owner here?" Greg spoke up answering, "Yes, I am Greg ."Hill looking around ask ,"Where is the couple?" Greg tells Feng to bring the couple to them. Lloyd recognizing Feng, got surprised and shouts out, "HEY!... REMEMBER ME FROM EARLIER?... THANKS AGAIN." Greg saw him go upstairs for the couple. And he became curious asking, "What happen earlier?... And, how did you know my name?" Lloyd then made eye contact with the bartender answering," We know Linda, she dates an officer is how… And, a Purse earlier was thrown at me… I didn't see a big knife coming… Your employee grabs me just in time. And it would've hit my heart, the guy saved life." Greg then understood. "And they all heard a siren sound from the outside.

Brain starts to laugh out loud covering his wounds. Lloyd thought his laughter was rather awkward asked, "What's funny?" He then saw the paramedic's come inside answers," Nobody seen where he went! I know we had a great crowd. But,... someone seen where he went." The paramedics now came, and after talking with the police, they took him to the ambulance. And the couple then met with the officers ready to be questioned. Feng had stood to the bar to view everything. Hill then saw his partner reach to his back pocket for a small notepad with a pin attached. Hill in a calmly manner says, "Officer Lloyd, will you question them for me... Greg, I want to talk to you alone." And they took a walk near the entrance, away from everyone. Hill now facing him says," This guy had a knife on him... Before you cover for your staff. You gotta ask yourself how, right?... What if he had a gun, right?" Greg understood, looking down with his arms crossed. And he in all seriousness says," We have to be extra sharp... Now, I only have one lead man." Hill nodded and says, "I think we understand each other." Hill then turned around, and asked Lloyd," Lloyd, did you get everything?" Lloyd writing everything down answered," Just about." Greg than said, "Your welcome to check our camera room upstairs." Hill then looks up at the office, and gave no expression says, "Of course we will." Greg then met with Feng, and gave him Brians position. And the bouncers all gathered around Feng, giving him praise. And the owner with the officers had left for the camera room. And they then spent an hour watching the footage that night.

    The next morning at the Police Department. Hill and Lloyd were seated in Sergeant Lewis's office explaining the club situation. Hill says, "It's like the guy wanted to prove himself or something. Lloyd, questioned the couple there.... Come to find out, the guy that saved my partners life works there." Lewis seated at his desk confuse ask," What do you mean, saved Lloyd's life?...

Where were you?" Lloyd and Hill begin to gaze at each other, for two seconds. Lloyd now clearing his throat answers," Hill shot the thug at the leg, and I was in front." Lewis still confuses, stopped the conversation by raising his hand asked, "How was a civilian involve in saving your life, Lloyd?... Tell me?" Lloyd looking down a little embarrassed, answers, "The civilian saw a big knife being thrown at me, and voluntarily saved my life.

Before Lewis could make a remark, a detective had knocked at the door. And he, wondering who it was asked," Who is it?" The detective answered," It Lugo." Lewis then smiled, liking his timing. And he told him to come inside the office, and introduces detective Lugo to them. And the detective, after closing the door, had stood next to Lewis. Lewis says," He had transferred to this station out of convenience... Lugo, is a very determined person from what I hear... And he is going to go undercover to join Steve Liang's gang... Were also keeping an eye on Powers too... I am now telling you both this... The detectives and I already had a meeting regarding this case... And I now want you two involved in the case." Lewis then focused on Lugo says,"... Lugo!... Two years ago, the last undercover detective became crooked. Officer Hill caught him selling drugs with a few members of the crew... Detective Miller was caught selling drugs at a gas station to detective Mary. And he refused the arrested and was killed a week ago, by her in self-defense... And it amazes me what make up, a blonde wig and some high heels can do." Lugo then smirked at the comment, watching the officers. Hill, being curious about the guy at the club last night, ask," How do you know this kid is in a gang, boss? Lewis then glanced at the detective answers," Lugo, do explain." Lugo nodded and says, "I've been taking pictures, and investigating Steve for the past two months. Steve the new crime leader or lord of the crime lives in the Suburbs of West haven... And how I found out about the new leader was by following, and overhearing the four women they sleep with... And I heard the name Richie spoken a few times also. This was outside a yogurt store at the time. And the young ladies seem to stick together from what I saw, and their faces are charted in the meeting room. Along with the pictures with them and the crew members... Steve stands at five feet seven, with a slim built. And he was once arrested for threating a police officer's family." Hill becoming impatient asked," So, the kid? ...." Lugo quickly interrupts answering," The kid last night at the club is named, Robbie Wong... Robbie is always seen with Steve at a wine store called, Wine Mind in New Haven on Howard Ave... It's owned by his aunt named, Maggie Liang... And the streets is how I found out about their relations." Hill tries to figure the detective out asked," So, you've been watching him on the low?" He answers," Yes indeed. I'm now involve with this case... I wanna take this man down for good... With your help of course." Hill nodded, and waited for him to continue on.

Lugo then continued says," Detective Mary had a word with Maggie and got nothing. Maggie owns two wines store and knows nothing about Steve's activities. And the manager among them is named Eric Miller... Maggie can be found at the Hamden store by the way. Now!... Steve Liang, alias Lord Liang... His brother named, Shawn Liang... Alias, Samyaza the demon of addiction was murdered. Shawn's girlfriend at the time named, Yonce. She, being disappointed in the affair, had spoken with Mary. And she said he tried to make peace with Powers, and she didn't know much more... Shawn had a warrant out for his arrest for drug trafficking and committing a bank robbery. And he was arrested once before, at the age of 18 for assault battery... And he also had stolen a rich guy's car, at an expensive restaurant... Now, back to the bank robbery. Shawn with two members named Jim and Eric, were also involved in drug trafficking... And they all of course wore ski masks... Shawn only escaped, and stole half a million.

One officer outside was shot by Eric from behind. And two cops inside the bank, had shot the two men due to self-defense... A total of three officers at the bank on Rose Street... Customers were on the ground watching at the time... Shawn had gotten unmasked fighting a cop on his way out, before being shot in the back... He then took off in a black SUV speeding. Thank God for the security cameras picking up everything... The day of his funeral I wasn't there but was told by detective Peter, that he got nothing... Peter was ignored by the family members." Hill in remembrance said," That robbery made news, I remember."

Lloyd being curious asked," Who killed his brother, and where is the money?" Lugo answers," The detectives and I believe someone from Powers did this. And we believe Steve has hidden the money. Shawn was having an affair with a married woman... And her name being Mrs. Susan Miles, was in Powers for about a year... Her husband named, Mr. Kirk Miles, had caught them in the act. Shots were fired, and calls were made to us according to Peter that afternoon... They remained married for a few months, and then had separated. Kirk supposedly was one of Powers best man... And their neighbor, being a friend to the wife, had told us that Steve had marked them for death... And that they are now living in Virginia... This was days after Mary had spoken with Susan. Their neighbor said they were seeing each other off and on then. Detective Mary already question Susan alone, and she admitted to having an affair with Shawn... Susan spoke about pocketing drug money, and being kicked out of Powers... Kirk remained a member regardless of her situation. And she also spoke about their gun range meeting area.... One of the members being the owner also... She doesn't know who. And when asked, where Shawn had gotten the drugs from, she never answered... I believe these two can help us out, in exchange for their protection... Sergeant Lewis said that he'd do his best in finding them... Detective Ronald is on the Powers case." Lewis then nodded in agreeance listening. Lloyd replies, "An affair? That makes sense and confirms it." Lewis now says, "Steve is after his brother's killer... Two days after the robbery, Shawn's body was found deep in the bushes, at the park on Jay street... This had happened two months ago in the park around 9:56 pm... Two shots to the back, and one in the head. No witnesses."

Lugo says," The cameras at the gas station on Lexington Ave, in the evening time gave us a Caucasian male. And he was wearing a gold necklace, black t shirt, blue jeans and a ski mask. And he drove close to Shawn and parked. The guy's necklace was broken and left on the ground... Shawn's fingerprints were all on the necklace. And this was due to the money from the bank robbery on the news, and revenge for the affair... The guy run up on Shawn pumping gas in his car from behind. Shawn was held at gun point, and asked about the money. And he said that he didn't have any money... And the guy with the gun, lastly said this is for Susan. Shawn turned around and said the name Kirk. And he caught him off guard, with a punch to the face. And the necklace broke as they wrestled. Shawn lastly tried to get a way, and need I say more... His body was taken inside a black SUV, and the killer left... Of course, we were called after this had happened. And the SUV was found near a construction site, on fire in North Haven."

Lewis now worried for Lugo says, "Lugo, you be careful, and thanks for saving this case. Lloyd and Hill will be your back-up if anything should go wrong. Terry will follow and record everything... Report back to me or the Caption like you should... Gentlemen, let's prove we can solve this, without the drug agency taking over... I'll let the captain know what's up, you're dismissed... And, Officer Lloyd and Hill, please!... no more being saved by a civilian, alright?... This is a Police matter!" They agreed and got up saying at the same time," Yes boss!"

Kirk that same hour had stop by at his ex-wife apartment in Virginia. And he wasn't over her and wanted to rekindle their relationship. And he wore a hat with shade to cover himself. Susan was in the living room, seated on the couch watching TV. And she heard the shaking noise from the doorknob. And he then begins to knock at the door a few times. Susan now became curious, shows up to the door asking," Who is it?" Kirk answers, "It's Kirk!... I think we should have a talk... I see you've changed the locks already?" Susan with her arms cross yelled, "YOURE NOT WECOME BACK HERE KIRK! I WAS ALREADY ASKED A QUESTION ABOUT YOU BY TWO DETECTIVES IN CONNECTICUT!... I WILL CALL THE COPS IF YOU DON'T LEAVE!" He immediately got upset with the remark and walked away. And he knew nothing of their conversation and felt worried. Kirk approaching his car thought about the two detectives. And he decided to go back, to live in New Haven C. T... Why, because there was no place like home.

Two hours later at the Feng residence. Lo stood in front of everyone around the TV, teaching the word of God in the living room. And the deacons, amazed, sat in front wanting to hear more word. Feng sat next to his mother behind the deacons, in thought about his life. Lo says," It's in Luke 8 verse 17 !... Nothing is hidden! Nothing is hidden that will not become evident! I hope you all get the message I am teaching you... It's all about secrets... May this come to the light for you all." Lo's eyes were now opened by the lord looking up. And he being amazed says," I have no idea why I am seeing two canary birds... I'm seeing a painting with these two birds... Like, representing two sisters or something." Lo then closed his eyes and said," Alright... Stand everyone... All eyes shut as we look to the Lord." Everyone stood with their eyes closed. And he then gave the benediction, and afterwards everyone began greeting each other. And the deacons were now making their way to the kitchen.

Polly looks at Feng being deep in thought asking, "Son, what's wrong?" Feng answers, "It's my job. I'm thinking about looking for another one." Polly feeling confused, replies, "I thought things were well at your job. You mention you wanted to become a manager there someday, right?" Before Feng could answer, his father came over wondering why they weren't in the kitchen eating. Lo asked," What's up?" Polly then looked at her husband out of concern for Feng. And she left them to conversate, and went into the kitchen. Feng disappointed says, "The lead guy was stabbed two times, by some punk, trying to touch another man's girl... It happened the night I got promoted as second lead, now I am first." Lo had waited for him to calm down. And when he did, lo asked, "You think this will happen to you, is what you're saying?" He nodded yes looking away. Lo notices it and says, "I don't like that you work at a club... It's a danger in my eyes... Your mother and I saw the news that night... What did the police say?" Feng answers, "They are looking into it.... My boss now has a gun for his protection." Polly then comes back into the living room getting Feng's attention by waving. And she said, "Angel is here!" Lo smiled at him saying, "I rather you not work there. But, if you do ....be careful son... And on that note, let's eat." Feng then chuckled at the remark asking, "What did mom make?" Lo watched her go back into the kitchen answers, "She wanted to surprise us, let's eat." And they came and ate her delicious traditional stew and enjoyed themselves.

Lugo, Hill, Terry and Lloyd met three hours later, at the entrance of the police department. And they came up with a plan for Lugo to get notice and join the crew. Lewis approved of the plan, and agreed to move that day. Terry then wired Lugo in the police van. And he gave him a wireless earpiece. And the earpiece size, was the size of a button to communicate.

15 minutes later, they arrived in the area and were in position. Hill with Lloyd had parked around the corner from the wine store, close to the police recording van. And the wine store was big inside and out, away from other buildings. And the inside had five aisles, a manager's office, a cash register, bathrooms and a receiving room in the back. And two cameras inside, at the front and back.

Lugo at the time, was glancing at the store by the entrances of an alley. And he was one building up, and across. And he was waiting for Steve to come out of the store. And the detective knew the car he drove around in, which was a black cutlass car parked in front. And they also knew the store owned by his aunt, was his normal hot stop. Steve didn't want to draw any attention whatsoever. Terry in the recording van, speaking to Lugo, says, "Lugo, remember… We only have one shot to make this clown believe your heartless." Lugo had seen the door open, and saw Steve. And he was smoking a cigarette, with three of his generals. And their names were Lucky, Robbie and Chi… Richie absent, was his number one general. And they were talking around the entrance. And there weren't many people around the area. Steve looking around, had told Robbie to go back inside. And the detective wore a black t shirt, with buttons around the collar, and pocket area where the mini micro spy camera was. And the camera itself, was the size of a button. And he being ready to move, in a cocky manner, says, "YO! YO! This is our guy!… I am going in." And he then touched the wire to adjust the camera. And he begins to walk toward Steve and the crew. Now, Steve had finished and dropped the cigarette, seeing him come near.

Hill with Lloyd had come around the corner like they had practice. And they came fast with their sirens on, and had stopped

Lugo. And the detective, had crossed the street and stood on the sidewalk. Steve watched the cops parked near and got out the car. And the crew wondered what was going on, watching the cops meet with Lugo. Lugo glancing at the officers says, "I didn't do anything, officers!" And they began to use intimidation, and got loud in his face. And he stood his grounds, being watched. Hill loudly asked, "WHY ARE YOU OVER HERE?" Lugo answers, "I just wanna buy some wine, man!... It's my girlfriend birthday... And, I wanted to surprise her." Lloyd sizing him up asked," Do you live around here?" Lugo then frowned, and felt they were being suspicious of him asked," What is this?... I'm I under arrest or something? "Hill not liking the attitude, says," Watch it sir! I got a bone to pick with you !" Lloyd then pushed him up against the car door. And he was acting surprised, arguably shouting, "WHAT'S YOUR PROBLEM!" Hill then reached for his gun and looked around. And he saw the crew staring back at them. And he believing, he got their attention shouts, "THERE'S NOTHING TO SEE HERE !"And he mean mugs Lugo, and walked away in a no-nonsense manner, saying, "You think your bad, don't cha!... You stay away from my sister!... Do you hear me !" Lugo with a confused look says," What?... Alright man! Take it easy!" Lloyd then looked around, and taps his partner on the arm, said, "Let's go." Lugo, moving away from the car, had saw them leave. And he, having the crew's attention, had gone into the wine store.

 Steve then tells Chi to watch Lugo, and the fellas were amazed at what just happened. And the detective at the time, was looking for white wine. And the manager was using the restroom, with the wine truck in mind. Lugo looked up, and saw he was being followed by the mirror in the aisle. And he immediately turned around facing him asked, "Hey!... Are you following me?" Steve heard and went inside with Lucky. And he with the fellas, had stood at the beginning of the aisle, and focused on him. Steve asked, "Do you bring cops with you everywhere you go?" Lugo facing them had spotted Robbie. And the cashier, a crew member, was watching him as well. And he was looking for a signal, with a gun around the register. Lugo quickly answers, "I'm on probation now... I got out a month ago for armed robbery. Those cops are watching me like you guys are... Are you guys' undercovers or something?" Steve then made eye contact with the cashier shaking his head no. And the cashier had put the gun away. Steve answered, "You should know a cop when you see one, as well as a Boss." He then glanced at the crew, and says, "Alright, leave him be." Lugo now takes a breather watching the guys exit out. And he wanting to gain more attention shouts out, "THE NEXT TIME I SEE THOSE COPS WILL BE THE LAST TIME!... I SHOULD HAD GOT WITH THE SISTER!" Steve heard, and looked at lucky at the entrance saying, I might need him for a job... Guys like him are hungry, and wouldn't mind making a fast buck... Take a picture of him, and tell him I want to see him. "Lucky did what he was told.

5 minutes later. Lugo, Chi and Lucky met with Steve behind the store. And he smiles at Lugo asked," You need a job?" Lugo, glancing at the fellas behind him answered," Yes... Who are you?" Steve had told the fellas, he wanted to talk with him alone. And the fellas had walked away, and stood to the side of the building. Now, all but one general had arrived, and parked at the back of the store. And one general had caught their attention, by waving them over to gossip. Steve then introduces himself, and told very little saying," I'm a businessman... A kind of violent businessman... But, I am good to my people." Lugo asked," What are you offering?... What kind of job?" And he answered," Watch man." Steve then spoke for a few minutes, about him earning his way up due to the lack of trust. And when he proves he can be trusted, he will become rich. So, he was now asked, does he agree

to join the crew. Lugo excited, had agreed says," You want your flowers now, right?" Steve then chuckled at the remark answers," Flowers?... No, Lugo... I deserve a garden for the lifestyle I can provide you." He then was told, that he would be taking orders from someone under him. And he asked for Lugo's number, and said that his lead would be in touch. And he then reach into his back pocket and handed him an untraceable phone, for contact. Lugo nodded and was dismissed. Chi shortly, had met with Steve asking," Well, what do you think?" He answers," It's hard to say right now. He will answer to you, from me... And if he fails me, you kill him, understood?" Chi had nodded yes, with a smirk on his face.

Later that evening, at a House music event at Jades. Feng with Greg were talking about being safe in his office. And the owner had two empty glasses on the desk, and was filling it with a bottle of club soda. And he walked from his desk with the drinks, and hands Feng one saying, "Feng, my friend. You have nothing to worry about... What happen to Brian, won't happen to you... I like your idea on tripling the security." Feng stood near the door in thought. And after finishing the soda, he saw a gun near the bottle. And he making conversation about it, said, "I see your packing." Greg looks at the gun finishing the soda. And he walks over to Feng, receiving the glass back answered, "I gotta protect myself as well, you know... Any other questions, Feng?" His phone starts to vibrate in his back pocket. And he reached, and saw it was Nia. Feng answered," I have no other questions." Greg then walked over to his desk and took a seat. And he placed the glasses down, and remembered he'd hired an Ast. Manager. Greg quickly replies, "Hey... I just hired an Ast. Manager named, Melissa... She will be starting soon. I will have a meeting with you all about it... I thought I could do it by myself, but anyhow." Feng heard him opening the door said, "Alright boss." Greg nodded watching him close the door.

That same hour at the Feng residents. Polly sat at the kitchen table with the lights off worried about Feng's safety. And her husband was in bed at the time alone. And he woke up not seeing Polly, wondering where she was. And he left the bedroom and entered the living room. And he heard a chair move in the kitchen. And the lights were off, so he checked and saw Polly. And she watched him turn the lights on, and sat with her. And she said, "I couldn't sleep." Lo worrying about her asked ,"Is it about Feng? Because we spoke about his safety at the club already... Polly, he's not a kid anymore." She still in thought says," It's just the parent in me.... Feng told me he was gonna look for another job." Lo then touched her hand as a sign of comfort and answers, "That's a good decision.... There so much prayer in his life... Feng will leave the job soon... Now, let's go to bed." Polly, feeling encouraged, smiled and kissed him. And they got up. and went to bed that evening.

Feng the next morning, drove to the Yung residents to pick Nia up for breakfast. And she came out of the house casually dressed, wearing dark shades locking the front door. And she met with him opening the car door for her, and went in. And he closed her door and got in the driver's seat. And he became curious, as to why he hasn't been inside the house, asked," When are you gonna let me come inside your house?... Your room, you know?" Nia watching him close his door answers, "My brother and I really don't get along. And... I don't want him starting with you, Feng." He now with a question, regarding her parents asked," Well, what about me meeting your parents... Am I gonna meet them, or?...." Nia hearing this, becomes annoyed, answers, "My parents are not together, but live in New jersey. You know this.... What's with all the questions?" Feng, avoiding the argument, looked ahead and started driving off to the restaurant. And he says, "I'm just trying to get to know you more... Lighten up, babe!" Nia with an attitude says, "Just drive, Feng!" And he indeed kept quiet til they arrived.

They now arrived at this uncrowded elegant restaurant, and got a table for two with the waiter's help. Nia then removed her shades and sat with Feng. And the waiter gave two menu flyers saying, "I will be with you guys in just two minutes." The waiter then went to the back room. So, he tries to get her in a good mood asking, "So, what can I do to make your day girl?" She then smiled, reaching for his hand near a basket of bread stick. And while blushing, to the left had saw her cousin Steve. And he was seated with two men in suits talking at the time. One man being a drug lord named Mr. Smith. The other gentleman, was his right-hand man named Cowell. And the meeting was to end their relationship, now that he is in charge. And she began to panic, putting her shades back on. Feng watched, and begins to have mix feelings about her behavior asked," Are you seeing someone?" The waiter then comes over and asking, "Are we ready to order?" And she stared at Feng, with her mouth wide open in shock of the comment. And she removed her hand from his, and in a concerned manner answers, "No! No! No!... I'm just not feeling well is all." And again, she looked over and saw them leaving. And she then began to relax, and saw that the attention was on her. And the waiter then gazed at Feng asking, "Sir, are you ready to order?" And he shook his head at her in confusion. And he glanced at the breakfast special answers," Let me get the pancake special with orange juice." And the waiter wrote the order down, now waiting for her order. Nia with the flyer, now answers, "I will have the pancakes as well with lemon water." And the waiter then walked away with their orders. And he stared back at her as she removed her shades again. And she wanting to cheer him up says," You always make my day, love... Are you working tonight?" He smiling at the remark, answers, "No, I don't... I'm thinking about quitting and becoming a I. T. guy... I've been having thoughts on settle down, and raise a family... I am thinking more future. "Nia was in all of what was said, and begin to smile asking," You want a future with me?" He watching the waiter come over to their table with their drinks answered," Yes." They then kissed.

Chapter 3

Detective Lugo was conversating with Lewis that afternoon, at the Police station outside his office. Lugo says, "Steve asked me to come work for him, and I said yes." Lewis staring at him for more info asked, "Doing what, and what do they call themselves?" He answered, "Being a watch dog for the cops. Steve never gave them a name from my understanding... Our plan worked!" Lewis then waves him to come inside the office. And he had opened, and closed the door. And they sat down. Lewis now using sarcasm says, "That's great, a no name gang... What if he asks you to kill someone? Also, was there any initiation?... And have you met the whole crew yet?" He given it some thought answers, "Almost everyone... No one with the name Richie yet... A man like Steve has generals, I mean …. He's Lord Liang, right?... I told him, I just got out of prison for armed robbery. His word was the initiation, boss... There are thirteen members not including the cashier." Lewis, gathering his thoughts says," The guy can't trust nobody... You know this, detective." He answered, "The fellas will know when to stop everything, to answer your killing question... I know I will be used and watched." Lewis in concern for the case says, "Avoid breaking any laws, detective." And the detective nodded yes, in agreeance. And the Sergeant looked over at a picture hanging to the left wall. And the picture showed himself, promoted Police Sergeant 10 years ago. And he immediately had thoughts of his glory days, and says, "I want this raid to be worth something, not anything stupid… That one and done, detective… Again, you be careful." Lugo then got up, ready to leave answered," Yes, sir."

And around that time at the wine store behind the building. Steve was in conversation with Chi and nine members. And, Chi was being told to text Lugo, that the orders would be coming from him. And that he needed to always be ready. Steve then receives a call from Richie, his right-hand man. And he, at the time was parked in front of a store. And he in a wicked manner says," Steve, you will never guest who I saw… I couldn't believe my eyes." Steve walked away pondering who asked, "Who?… And, where are you?" Richie answered, "The guy that killed your brother is on green street at a corner store, where I am… What do you want to do?" Steve then began to smirk answering," Bring him, and meet me at your mechanic shop!" The crew was ready for whatever. Steve then hung up, and faced the fellas saying, "Let's go for a ride." And they all, immediately got into their cars, leaving. And the manager, then opened the back door, not liking what he saw. And he was ready to call and complain to Maggie about it. Eric wasn't too fond of their company.

Richie at the time, was coming out of the car and saw no one present. And he goes inside the store, with a gun tucked under his shirt, looking for Kirk. And after passing a customer, he found him by the cooler, among few customers getting a soda. He gets behind Kirk, with the gun pressed to his back. And he in a sarcastic manner said, "Don't even try it." Kirk then drops the soda, and they came out of the store together. And the people around had seen, and some with children had turned away. Kirk being scared for his life, had asked, "What do you want man?"

And they came to the driver side, of Richie's car. Kirk, now at gun point, was forced in, closing the door. And he came in, and sat at the passenger seat closing the door. And he had aimed the gun to his waist, saying, "You will find out soon enough, now drive." Kirk indeed drove 15 minutes to the mechanic shop. And he then, regretted coming back home.

And they arrived at Richie's mechanic shop, and had parked in front. And he saw the lights on inside, with only three cars in the parking lot. And the shop size was half the size of a supermarket, away from other buildings. And inside there, was an auto repair area, a customer service desk and Richie's office behind the desk. And the customer service desk had a sign showing closed, with no one present. Kirk, not understanding the whole situation had asked, "Why are we here ?" Richie was now on the phone calling Steve. And he answers," Listen, Richie... You stay outside, and bring him to the repair door!" Richie answered, "Alright." And he tells Kirk to get out the car, and he got out. And he was being forced again, at gunpoint to the door. And when they arrived at the door, he opened and pushed kirk inside, closing it shut. Kirk immediately saw Steve, standing with the crew in the middle of the repair area. Steve staring at him asks," Why you kill my brother?" Kirk stepping back frightened, had asks, "Your brother?... Who?" And they all saw him at the door shaking the knob. Steve then waved at Lucky for a gun, says, "You knew he was my brother, didn't you?"

Kirk, facing him again, had gotten on his knees begging for mercy. And he asked, "How did you know it was me?" He then looked to the left, and saw a close friend of his named Roy. Kirk confused had asked," Roy, why are you here?... Are you with Steve?" Roy nodded yes and said," It was a foolish idea, Kirk."

Richie at the time, was watching the cars go by. And he heard five shots fired at kirk. And there were two in the stomach, and three in the chest. And his body had fallen back from the impact, hitting to the door hard. And there was blood all around him. And their boss wipes the gun with his shirt, and hands the gun back to Lucky. Lucky then kept the gun behind his waist, awaiting orders. And he had the crew clean the blood, leaving no trace.

10 minutes later, a supervisor named Jane Garcia had drove by the shop. And she had viewed everything, including Richie on his phone. And she, with her phone charger on her mind, thought to come through the back door. And she parked in the back, and showed up to the back door with the key. And she, giving it no thought, had opened and closed it. And the crew had seen her, and a man named Sunny immediately ran, and grabbed her. Jane tried to wrestle him but couldn't. And she was in shock, witnessing everything, and begin to close her eyes. Sunny then glanced at Steve asking ," Boss?" Steve saw, and knew that she was frightened asks," You have a key to the back door?... Who are you?" She calming down, from being in the state of shock answers," I'mma supervisor!... I... I just work here!... Please, please don't kill me mister." Steve then waved to Lucky and was handed the gun again. And he begins to smile at her, saying," Your fate is in my hands!... I leave no witnesses !" And she screamed out loud and was shot in the heart. And with attitude, he glanced at Sunny asking," You didn't think to cover her mouth, Sunny?" And he was surprised, that Steve had fired, facing her, held by him. Sunny, feeling awkward answers," Boss, you had asked her a question." And their attention was caught by the front door opening. And they saw Richie come in asking ," I heard a woman scream, boss? "And he saw the body of the supervisor with Kirk's. And he wondering how, had asked," How?... Where did she come from?" Steve given no expression answers," I guess you gave her a key to the back door... Who was she ?... I can't have any witnesses, Richie. "Richie surprised answered," Her name was Jane, and she

was my supervisor. "Steve then gathered the fellas. And he had the crew continue to clean, and lock all doors. Richie was told to guard again, with the thought of Jane's death. And he knew that the situation was out of his hands. So, he thought of a distraction to ease his mind. Now, 13 minutes had passed, and one person came to mind by texted. So, he begins to text.

Steve then opened the door and saw Richie texting away. And he told him to destroy the footage, and had closed the door back. Richie heard, and was in the middle of texting a beautiful woman named Jasmine. Now, Jasmine would normally hang around the crew from time to time. And she, being a gold digger, was distracting him. And she had texted, I want you now capitalized. Richie had seen the door open again. And the crew with the bodies, were now leaving. And two men at the time, were putting the bodies in a trunk. Steve, ready to leave, had words with Richie. And the crew then left to get rid of the cars and bodies. Richie, now caught up in lust, immediately texted her back, I'm leaving now. And after locking up, he left for Jasmine's apartment forgetting what was said. That evening, the crew had buried the bodies, deep in the wood in New Haven.

Lugo later that evening, showed up at the wine store to get more info. And he then opened the door, and saw a clean cut, naked faced tall young man. And he was in conversation with the cashier, at the checkout area.

And he was talking to the cashier who was a crew member about kirk. Lugo had no idea this was Richie. And the manager was in the back room receiving wine at the time. And the cashier looks at Lugo asking, "See any cops? "He answered, "No, I haven't." Now, Richie had never met Lugo before. And he curiously asked, "Who are you?" The cashier answered, "He's Steve's watch dog, Richie… You didn't know that?... Lugo, this is Richie." Lugo was now surprised, to have finally met him. Richie had laughed at the thought of him being a watch dog. And after calming down from laughter, he says, "So, you must have heard that Steve had avenge his brother, right?... Wait, you weren't there." Lugo then walk closer to him asking, "Who?... Steve, kill someone." Terry at the time was parked near, listening to their conversation while drinking coffee.

Richie looks around the store and quietly answers," A guy named Kirk had killed his brother months ago. And his mistake, was not knowing his friend Roy was working for Steve... Kirk wanted Roy's help, to kill Shawn... Shawn at the time, was trying to stop gang violence... Now, Kirk's dead, deep in the woods in New Haven." Lugo, wanting to better understand him asks, "He kill him in the woods?" Richie again looked around and saw nobody. And he answers," We met at my mechanic shop on Long Ave... I am the owner... He did him there, and buried him in the woods.... Well, him and a girl too... My only supervisor." Lugo, making sure he heard him right asks," A girl?... Who?" Richie then regrets bringing her up, begins to leave. And he had stopped at the door, giving their conversation some thought. And he faced Lugo, says, "Watch dog, you say?... Glad you're with us, your name again?" Lugo answered," It's Lugo... Chi tells me what to do, which is watch." He nodded and said," You'll be taking order from me very soon... Nice meet you, Lugo." Richie then left.

And the detective glanced at the cashier asking," Did he say how deep in the woods?" The cashier then raised his hands asking," These question, why?" Lugo in a sarcastic manner answers," Hey!... I'm the watch dog, right?" The cashier then stares at him for a few seconds, reply," Somewhere north, on Indian trail ave, deep in the wood is all I know... Richie, I tell ya... He should learn to keep his mouth shut sometimes." Lugo now having thoughts of the girl, had asks," He said a girl too, right ?... Who? "The cashier then became very annoyed by the questions. And he in an annoyed state, answers ," A girl had walked in on the action was all !... Jane was her name. He had spoken about her, ten minutes before you came... That poor girl. "Lugo immediately backed off. And he exits the store, with no sign of the crew. And he heads to his car to relax. And after opening the car door, he sat down giving the whole conversation some thought. And he spoke into the wire asking," Did you get that?" Terry, gathering his thoughts, answered yes. Terry then begins to call the murder in.

Nia that same evening, was in her room thinking about Feng. And she reached for the phone on the bed, with a mind to call Brenda. And she called, wanting to be given some good advice. Brenda answers, "Hello, Nia?... How's everything?" Nia began to walk back and forth around her bed in thought. And she stopped and answers, "I'm doing, ok." Brenda at the time, was home in the kitchen, finishing the dishes. And she held the phone, using her face and shoulder. And she begins to wonder, what was on her mind had asked, "How's the relationship, girl?" Nia then sat on the bed replies," I don't know really... He questions me on a lot of things, Brenda." Brenda then turns the sink off, and dries her hands with a towel near the sink. And after they had dried, she threw the towel away, and sat at the table. Brenda then became curious asking, "Questions like, what's your favorite color or?" Nia quickly answers, "No... He wants to get to know my family, and I don't want him to... Definitely, not after that huge argument between my father and Alex 3 years ago... There is a lot of bad things like pride, acholic behavior and abusiveness." Brenda then understood, but wanted to make a point asked, "Is he wrong for wanting to get to know your family?... Or, do you think your folks won't approve of him?" Nia takes a breather and answers, "They will like him... My father was abusive, and my brother can be also... I just wish my family were perfect." Brenda then, in a mild tune voice says, "Give this man a chance, he sounds like a good guy... Nia, you're always giving these bad boys a chance... Have you ever considered this man's feeling?" Nia then reaches for her teddy bear near the pillow. And, after giving it some thought, she finally realized Brenda was right. And she answers, "Your right, Brenda... Feng does care for me... He isn't like the jerks I have been with. "Brenda then smiled saying," Maybe the next time you call me, you'll be engage." Nia then begun to lay on her bed, in thought of the remark. And she held the teddy bear very close to her heart, still in thought. And after their conversation, she felt at peace and called it a night.

The next morning at the Feng residents. Feng wakes up to a call-in bed avoiding the call. And after a few minutes had gone by, he reached to the drawer nearby and saw it was Nia. And he answers, rubbing his eyes asking, "What's up?" Nia was in the bathroom touching up her eyebrow's. And she in a sweet manner voice said, "I thought about you last night." Feng surprised, had sat up alert. And he tries to have a better understanding, replies," You thought about me?... Like, something good or...?" She laughs at the comment and answers, "Good of course, Feng... I want to see you, are you busy?" He answers," I just woke up." And he heard her giggling at him.

And her brother, from downstairs, had come to the door and started knocking. And she heard and said," Feng, I will call you back." And she hung up, and sat down the razor near the sink coming out. And she then threw her phone at the bed, and opened the door asking, "What is it?" Alex smirking answers, "It's dad, he wanted to speak with you... The house phone is at the counter near the sink... Why is your door lock?" She then ignored him, and went downstairs for the phone. And she with the phone answered, "Dad?....." And their father named Fei Yung, was seated at the deck of his house at the time. And he asked, "Nia, how is everything?" Nia not in the mood, with an attitude answers, "Dad, I don't have any money!" And he got unset, and loudly asked, "YOU THINK I CALLED YOU FOR MONEY?" Fei had waited for her responds, but she remained quiet. And he now, in a soft tune voice reply, "Listen, I will pay you back… This time I promise… I haven't gambled or had a drink in years." She immediately hung up, and slammed the phone down disappointed. And her brother heard the noise and came into the kitchen. And he saw Nia with her arms crossed with tears streaming. And he having some idea curiously asked," He ask you for money, right?" Nia then walked away upset, yelling," WHY DOES THIS HAVE TO BE MY FAMILY!" And he watched her go back upstairs, hearing the door shut. Alex didn't know what to think, regarding their conversation.

Lugo that same morning, was parked in a restaurant parking lot. Terry was across the street, in the van watching. They had followed Roy to a restaurant, and waited for him to finish breakfast. Roy was spotted earlier at a stop light on red. And the detective saw and immediately called Terry to follow. And he had a few questions in mind, to better help the case.

45 minutes later, he came out of the restaurant in a rush. And the detective saw, and got out the car to meet with him. And he then met up from behind shouting, "YO, ROY!" Roy now stopped, and faced him near his car. And he, recognizing him by a picture, begun to smirk says," I didn't even see you, man… That's right, you're the watch dog." They then greeted each other with a handshake. And the detective catching him in a good spirit, softly says," I heard Steve got the guy, man." Roy was caught off guard by the remark. And he became curious, looking around asking, "So, you heard things are well now…. Who told you that?" Lugo quickly answers, "Richie, why?… I'm the watch dog, bro… Come on!" Roy then nodded, and let his guard down a little. Lugo saw

and quickly says," I'm hungry, but let me ask you.... Steve got him and the girl, right?... And who was the girl?" Roy thought the questions was awkward answers, "Yes, I was there... Are you conforming with me?" Lugo then, in an insecure manner said," Yeah, I wasn't there." Roy thought the comment was rather odd but answers," Steve, finally got what he wanted.... And the girl was a supervisor. Wrong place at the wrong time was all... What's with all the questions, man?... Wait, you weren't there to see it." Lugo laugh and says, "I wasn't there to see the gangster in him, you know what I mean... I look up to you guys, and hope to lead someday is all." Roy now, looking out for him in a serious manner says," Lugo, you're not supposed to ask me these kinds of questions... You ask those questions to who you report to only, got it?" He nodded yes and said," Alright, man!" They then parted ways.

Lugo then came in the restaurant and stood near the entrance to watch him leave. And after he left, he walked back to his car to call Hill. And the officer was patrolling with Lloyd in the West Haven area at the time. And he approaches a stop light on red, receiving the call. And he saw the number and answered," Lugo, what cha got for me?" Lugo then opened his car door, and sat in answers, "Steve just killed a guy and girl. Richie, a cashier crew member, and Roy are saying the same thing... I gotta to tell Lewis." Hill had saw the light had turned green reply," Let him know, and thanks for the update."

Lloyd finally remembers where he knew Feng from says, "Hey. That civilian that saved me... We when to school together. I knew I seen him from somewhere, I didn't know his name then." Hill nodded, now making a left turn, coming into the parking lot of police Department says, "He's another one that should become a cop." And when they came inside, they were in Lewis's office given a report. Lugo with Terry, had come to the office twenty minutes later.

Now, the bodies were found two days later, and the police had raided Steve's house. And the house was 4000 square feet, with three floors in the suburbs. And the police had found nothing, and thought it was odd. Steve at the time was in a warehouse in the main area watching the news. And the news left him feeling suspicious of his own gang. And he then knew that he couldn't go back home, and needed to kill who had told. And the news reporter at the gate of his house says," I have spoken with the Sergeant , and was told this... There is a warrant out for Steve Liang's arrest due to the murders. The murders of Kirk Miles and Jane Garcia. Jane, was a 19-year-old supervisor that worked at the mechanic shop on Lane Ave... Kirk was a member from the biker gang called Powers." As the news reporter spoke, a head shot of Steve Liang, known as Lord Liang, appeared on the screen... He continued to say, "If you see him, you should call the police ."

Mary and Peter were now assigned to watch Steve's house and report back. And they did what Lewis had asked, but witnessed no vehicle during their time of watch.

Vin watched the news at home on the living room couch. And he got up, and went into the kitchen for beer upset shouts, "YOURE A DEAD MAN, LIANG!... YOU BETTER WATCH OUT!" And his girlfriend named Wendy, had come out of their room, being curious. And she overhears him, asking, "What's that?" Vin had opened and closed the refrigerator with beer. And he opened the can and took a sip said, "Kirk's body was found today." Wendy then became upset and loudly dramatic. And she replies, "OH MY GOD, VIN! WHAT'S GOING ON HERE?" Vin finishing the beer, throws the can into a garbage can. And he then came back to sit on the couch again. And he out of aggravation and pressure answers, "How should I know!... I believe Liang had something to do with it... You remember the affair, don't cha!" Wendy answers, "I do, what's your plan?" Vin says, "All we need is someone or something to bring him out to kill him." She now walked over sitting next to him, becoming worried for his safety replies," I don't want you to be next.... So, if you see him, you finish him." Vin then smiled, putting his arm over her, and continued to watch the news.

Early that afternoon at Jades, the bouncers were gaining more hours coming in early. And they needed to make sure the night of the Reggae event was safe. And the cleaning crew and roadies were there also. Greg at the time was in the restroom. And the head bouncer" Feng "was giving out orders, and had received a text message from Nia. And he then gazed at his coworker named Tylor, near the DJ table doing nothing. And he saw the wrong speaker on top of the table says," Tylor, put the speaker away from the DJ table... It's the wrong speaker." And he walked outside, from the back door receiving the call. Tylor felt he was being told to do too much, as compared to everyone else. And he reached, and held the speaker aggravated. And with an attitude, he drops it. And the bouncers all saw, and had gotten worried. Angel saw that the speaker wasn't damage asks, "Tylor, you ok?" Tylor then takes full advantage, of the attention being on him shouted," WHY IS FENG ASKING ME TO DO EVERYTHING!" Angel quickly answers, "What do you mean? Jason, over to your left moved three speakers by himself... Tom Tom, had cleaned the mess from last night around the bar. What's your deal?" Tylor ignoring the remark asked, "Where is Feng?" Angel then pointed at the back door replies, "He on break outside, why?... Didn't you see him leave?" Tylor then left, to meet with Feng.

Feng was with Nia taking a picture, using her camera. And they, out of excitement, had begun to kiss around her car across the street. Tylor had seen, and looked both ways. And he had crossed to meet with them. And she, putting the camera on top of the car, saw Tylor. And immediately got Feng's attention by pointing behind him. And he faced Tylor with a frown asking," What are you doing out here?... I'm on break?" Then Tylor met with them, giving no answer asked," Why are you given me most of the work?" Feng now felt confused and awkward. And he not understanding Tylor answers, "I don't understand, I hardly ask you to do two thinks for me... What's wrong?"

Nia then tried to reason with him says, "Feng is a good guy!... He wouldn't boss you around." Tylor already frustrated, looked at her shouts, "WHY DON'T YOU SHUT UP, AND MIND YOUR BUSSNESS LADY !" Feng, not liking the disrespect, immediately got in his face. And with an attitude, he loudly asked, "WHAT'S YOUR PROBLEM, MAN!" Tylor argued, "Why should I do all the work is my problem!... I should go to Greg about this!" Nia then got in between them, as they continued arguing. Feng then yelled," YOU DONT WANNA DO ANY WORK IS YOUR PROBLEM!" And his coworker in a violet manner shouts," WHO DIED AND MADE YOUR GREG!"

Now, Greg had come out of the restroom, and saw everyone finishing up. And he immediately noticed that Feng and Tylor weren't present. And he becomes curious asking," Anyone seen Feng or Tylor?" Angel from the right side of the stage, holding two microphones answered, "Feng is on break... Tylor wanted to talk with him." And the owner heard, walking to the entry door to open it. And when it opened, he saw Tylor pushing Feng up against a car. Greg, now closing the door shocked, had waved to get their attention. And he yells," HEY!... STOP IT!... WHAT'S GOING ON, TYLOR!" And they all saw Greg and stopped. And she saw a small dent on her car, and became upset. And she out of frustrated had shouted, "REALLY, THAT'S MY CAR!" Tylor then met with Greg in the middle of the street, and tries to explain the whole situation. And the owner raised his hand to stop him from talking said," You're fired!" Tylor then paused for a few seconds. And he, in a confused state of mind had asked, "Why?... Feng was having me do everything, Greg!" And the owner in a no-nonsense manner answers, "Feng's the lead man on break! And, what makes matters worst is that you attack him in front of a witness... You're fired!... Now, grab your things and go!" Tylor then went back inside to get his belongings. Now, Greg, looking both ways, continued to cross, to make sure they were alright. And he saw the dent on the passenger side door. Greg in concern asked, "You want to press charges on him?" And she putting the camera inside the car answered, "No... Everything is fine sir, thank you." Greg then apologized to them, and offered to pay for the damage. And she then agreed to the offer.

30 minutes later, on the other side of New Haven. Roy was coming out of his apartment, and had been followed by Detectives. Detective Peter and Mary were waiting for him, parked across the street. And they saw him, and quickly got out of the car, closing their doors. And his attention was called by name. And he turned around and gazed at them asking, "Who are you two?... And how do you know my name?" They then held their badges and met with him. And detective Peter answered, "This is Detective Mary and I Peter, come with us sir... We have some questions for you." Roy then came with the detectives to the police department. And he didn't know what to think.

Chapter 4

Lugo and Lewis later that day, were arguing in his office about him sending other detectives. He felt that the detectives speaking to Roy, was way too early, and that it may blow his cover. And the sergeant seated at his desk, had watch the detective pace back and forth, reply," Lugo, sit down and listen to me." Lugo then took a seat, waiting for Lewis to speak. And he says, "I don't want this to turn into a cold case... That's my reason why more detectives are involved... I have Mary and Peter, watching Steve's house... So, I know who comes in and out. And he had murdered his brother's killer, and Miss Garcia... Steve has a warrant for his arrest now... You gave us Roy, as an eyewitness to the murders. And you told us where the bodies were... right?... So, detective what more do I need?" Lugo replied, "Your right about a warrant for Steve arrest... But, what about the money from the bank?... I feel there is another money source but what, right? They ain't out here robbing banks anymore... I also feel you moved too fast on getting Roy, after I just had question him... What about my cover you know?" Lewis with a question in mind had asked," Detective, tell me what goes on around the wine store." Lugo answers," They hang out, and are given orders by Chi or Richie, from Steve for anything... Believe me, they aren't crazy about wine at all… And they do go out to parties with women and such… But, I am told to stay at the wine store." Lewis then leans his head back on the seat. And he being in thought of the arrest, saying, "Your still apart of his gang, Lugo… You see him, you arrest him. You understand me?… I am sure after his arrest, he will speak about their money source." Lugo knowing this would put him at a risk reply, "Yes sir." He then got up worried. And he opened, and closed the office door.

And he met with the two detectives in the hallway. And out of curiosity he asked, "Did you guys get anything?" Mary with Peter had looked at each other, then focused on him. Mary answered, "We did… Roy is saying he kill Kirk, not Steve." Lugo had frowned, knowing it was a lie says, "He's covering for Steve… Our conversation was recorded. You know this, right?" Peter feeling lied to, had thought on the recording, replies, "He is looking at 25 or more, years to life !… Why would he want that is beyond me, unless some kind of deal was made… We'll have another chat with Mr. Roy then." And they all then parted ways.

Lugo then walked out the department, with the thought being why is he covering for Steve." His thoughts, lead him to go and check the cameras at the shop. And the sergeant opened the entry door and saw him, shouts," HEY!… LUGO!… IT'S A GOOD THING I CAUGHT YA !" Lewis saw that he had gotten his attention says," Listen, Terry will be following you again for the recording… Call him, and be safe." And the detective with an idea asked," Hey boss?… Would you so happen to have two hundred bucks on ya?… I'll pay you back." Lewis not understanding why replies," Why do you need two hundred?… You a little low with the rent?" Lugo had nodded yes, watching him reached into his back pocket, and met with him saying, "I better get this back, Lugo… I'm in the middle of a divorce." And he receives the money saying," Yes, sir!" And he watched the sergeant go back inside.

Lugo then crossed the street to the parking lot, and stood to his car. And he went inside the car to open the glove compartment. And he grabs a small crowbar tool near the recording wire. And he walked over to the front side window, and started to bash it. And he afterwards had bashed the other side too. And the cops going in and out of the department saw and were confused. And they all began to gossip, and saw the glass all around him. He then glanced at the officers, acting frustrated shouting, "NOT A GOOD TIME YOU GUYS!" And he then puts the crowbar back, and wired himself. And he closed the glove compartment back, calling Terry. Terry then understood where to meet him and why. And after the phone call, the detective takes off to the mechanic shop.

And when he arrived at the shop, there was one car being serviced by two mechanics. And he got out of the car, just in time to see the van parked. Terry was in the van parked close, and across the street from the shop. And the detective walks inside the shop and met with the mechanics. And he, now receiving their attention, had asked for Richie. And the mechanics thought he needed a job. And one of the mechanics had pointed to the customer service desk, says, "The boss, is over there… Was there anything else I could help you out with?" He replies," Thanks, I'm good." Lugo then came over to the desk, and saw Richie with Steve talking. And they were outside the office, and surprised to see him. Richie asked, "Lugo, what's up?" Steve had stared at him, with his arms crossed reading his body language. And he watched them greet each other with a handshake, with his righthand man asking, "What you need, bro?"

Steve, avoiding the conversation, had gone into the office, closing the door shut. And he answers," I need my two side windows replaced. Can you believe that… I don't know who did this… How long will it take?" And he, waiting for an answer, looked up to see where the cameras were. Richie now recognizing his car, through the big window in front answers," Not long, I got you… Grab a seat… So, you don't know who did this? Where were you at the time?" He smirked and answered," Home, sleep." Richie then shook his head at the situation, going into the office closing the door. And the detective stood looking inside the auto repair area from a distance. And he seen a camera near the tires and batterie area. Richie then opened the door and caught him looking. And he thought it was awkward, calling him to the office. And the detective enters in, and notices a video surveillance system near the desk. And he was now told to have a seat by Steve. And their boss was seated at the desk, looking at Richie at the time. And he softly said," Close the door, Richie." And he closed the door. He then focused on Lugo saying, "I am sure you heard the news about me, right?" Lugo nodded yes and answered," Yes, I have." Steve being in thought of Roy, asked," Have you seen Roy?" He answers, "Last time I saw him was at a restaurant… He was leaving, and I was going in." Steve out of curiosity, had made eye contact with Richie. And he got up, and slowly walked over to Lugo. And he, being deep in thought says, "The streets told me that two officers came for him… I also heard the cops had found the bodies… Someone's talking is my point, and I didn't say it was you… But, you're new." Now, his righthand man, with a question regarding Roy's loyalty had asked, "You think Roy will give you up, boss?" Steve had laugh at the comment and answers, "He's too loyal to the game… Alright, I am going to lay low for a while… Richie, you find out who told… and have them killed." And he replies," Yes, sir!"

Steve then told Lugo to leave the office. And he shortly had left, to live in a vacant warehouse he'd used from time to time. And they had no idea the wire was picking up on everything. And his car was fixed 33 minutes later without charge. And he kept the money and left. And the recorded conversation was reported back by Terry. And he was questioned by Lewis, why wasn't the arrest made. Terry answered that the detective could better answer that question. And the sergeant indeed, had kept that question in mind.

That evening, at Jades was the reggae event. Feng had given orders, with a team of three in each corner of the main hall. Now, around the stage a fight had broken out between two women. And he from a distance had heard, and saw the people moved aside. One was blonde, and the other a brunette. And they were attacking each other on the floor. Feng then met with them saying, "Ladies! Ladies!... Get a hold of yourselves." Angel then shown up, and held back the blonde on top. And he reached, and grab the brunette from the floor. And he saw that she had a black eye, and wanted to continue fighting. Angel asked," Why?" The brunette answered," She spill her drink on my shirt, and I told her off!" Feng glanced at them says, "It sounds like an accident to me." And the blonde had shouted," SHE SHOULD HAD WATCH WHERE SHE WAS GOING!" And he looks at the blonde and says," You can apologize outside, I got a job to do." And the ladies were now being removed from the club by Angel.

Angel had watched the ladies as they exit out. And the blonde out of aggravation says, "I am not apologizing to you! I'm not at fault!" Feng was waving them away, signing to keep it moving. And he noticed, that this was the third fight that had happened that evening. And he, immediately felt a hand on his right shoulder. Feng then turned around, and faced another bouncer named Luke. And he being frustrated had said, "A fight broke out at the entrance... What you want to do, tell Greg?" Feng began to take a breather and answers," I'm come now!... Is it the ladies?" Luke walking with him said," No." Feng had told him to stay inside, in case another fight happiness.

Now, two guys outside the club were being separated by two bouncers named Tom Tom and Jason. And threats were being issued out, because of a girlfriend cheating. And the girlfriend was laughing at the situation, while drunk saying, "What if I wanted you both!... What if!... Ha. Ha. Ha. Ha." And the girlfriend immediately made a sour expression due to the alcohol. And she held her stomach and began to vomit. And the crowd waiting to get into the club, had turned their heads out of disgust. And a bouncer named Tom Tom, in a sarcastic manner said," Oh, that's just great... That's beautiful." Feng coming close to the entrance saw, and met with Greg. And the owner was armed, with his phone on his mind says, "I left my phone in the car rushing here late tonight... I'll be back." Feng heard, and to the right saw a cop car parked. And the owner slowly moved, to watch how he would handle the situation.

And he noticing, he was being watch says," You guys go home, or I will tell the cop that's parked!... It's your choice!" Greg then began to rush to the left where his car was. And he looked both ways, and crossed the street going down one block. And he further down, had glances across the street, and saw Robbie talking to a woman. Greg recognizing him, yelled, "HEY! YOU WERE IN MY CLUB!... YOURE A WANTED MAN, YOU STAY THERE!" Robbie, not knowing who he was, starts to panic. And the lady became nerves, and quickly walked away from him. And he frowned asking, "Who are you?" Now, Robbie saw him quickly reach for something behind his waist. And he being quicker, had reached for his gun from behind, and fired three shots at Greg. And Greg immediately drops the gun, falling in pain. And he was in shock watching himself bleed. And they all heard the shots fired outside the club. And the men that were separated had went their own ways. And the guy she cheated with; felt she wasn't worth it had left. And the boyfriend, still in love, had remained with her. And the girlfriend then sobered up, with her hand to the mouth. And the couple were now across the street, in shock. And she removes her hand, shouted," OH MY GOD!" And the bouncers were immediately concerned for Greg. Now, Feng looking in Greg's direct shouts, "GREG!... GREG!" Now, Robbie heard and wanted to avoid the trouble. And was about to meet and ask a question, but ran away. And the owner was left in the middle of the street bleeding. And he had two bullets on the right arm, and one on the left shoulder. And Feng, and two bouncers had run to his rescue. And the owner within minutes, had seen them coming. And he also heard a police siren down the street. And they met with him, and saw the cop car coming their way. Now, Tom Tom saw the gun. And he glanced at Feng, in a confused state says, "Feng, look!... He used his gun." He saw and answered, "Self-defense!... Give me a hand, Tom." And he helped Feng with Greg.

15 minutes later the ambulance, and more Police came. Feng, and the bouncers had everyone leave due to the affairs by Greg. And the owner was laid out on the stretcher relaxing with two paramedic's. And the officer that was parked close to the club was named Collazo. And he at the time, wanted to know what had happened, so he asks, "Who else is in charge of the club?" Feng then met with him, away from the bouncers answering, "I am the lead guy, Greg is the owner." Collazo then asked, "Can you tell me what had happen?... What's your name sir?" He answers, "It's Feng... I was with these two guys to the left, TomTom and Jason... We heard the shots fired." Collazo then asks, "Did you see who drew their weapon first?"

Tom Tom quickly answered, "No!... We saw he was in the middle of the street bleeding. His focus was to the left side."

Collazo then looks at the bouncers, and Greg going inside the ambulance. And he says, "They both had guns... If it was

Greg that drew first… It doesn't look good for him at all… We will question him also, just a few more questions fellas." Collazo then from behind, had heard familiar voices in conversation. And he faces them, and sees Lloyd with Hill. And they had come from across the street, and met with him. Hill curiously asks, "What happen now?… We were passing by." Collazo then goes over what was said. Lloyd, hearing him out, looked over and saw Feng. And he says," So, none of these bouncers saw who fired first? And, where they were standing?" Collazo says," I am getting to that… The owner was laying in the middle of the street… The guy that shot him must have been towards the left side. The owner's body was turn more to the left… Two bouncers help him up… And I at the time, drove down to meet with them."

Lloyd then walks around the entrance of the club leaving the conversation. And he glanced four buildings down to the right, and saw a pizza shop. And he gazed at Feng asking, "Do you remember me?" Feng with a confuse look, stare at him asked, "Should I know you?" Lloyd begins to chuckle at the remark. And his attention was now caught by a bouncer mean mugging him. And Angel had mean mugged him, in fear that the club would shut down began to shout, "INSTEAD OF TALKING TO HIM, YOU SHOULD BE LOOKING FOR THE MAN WHO SHOT THE OWNER!" And the bouncers were all in agreement. Lloyd ignoring the remark, had pointed to Feng says, "We were in class together in middle school." Feng then glance very hard, and realizes who he was replies, "Chase?" Lloyd smiled, and walks over to him saying, "It's a small world isn't it." Feng catching on to his character answered," It is indeed." He then begins to rub his stomach looking at the pizza shop again. And he says, "I am hungry for a slice of pizza… Feng, you want a slice? It's my treat?" Feng knew then, he wanted to talk alone. And Angel not catching on says, "What If I or the others wanted a slice too?" Feng then walked away from the bouncers saying, "I'll be back." And they begin to walk to the pizza shop. And his partner saw and wanted to know asked,"Lloyd, what's this?" Lloyd smiled and said," I'll be back."

And a news reporter and crew had arrived. And they had parked across the street, making their way to the club. And the police saw, and weren't ready to deal with them yet.

Lloyd and Feng then showed up, and went inside an uncrowded pizza shop looking at the menu. Lloyd asks, "What kind of pizza do you like?" Feng in a no-nonsense manner, quickly asked," What's the real reason, you wanted to talk to me?... I don't want any pizza." Lloyd then looks at the teenage cashier saying," Two slices of cheese, with a bottle of water to go... Guy saves my life, and doesn't want nothing to eat at least?" Feng and the cashier had laughed at the remark. Feng reply, "I see, you don't have to do this Chase... Tonight, has been really crazy with the fights, and now Greg... We might be close until he gets better." Lloyd had thought about the comments made, waiting for his order. And he three minutes later, receives his order. And he starts to eat while being watched by the cashier. Feng understandings the cashier asked," Chase?... You forgetting something?" Lloyd in a joking manner answered," Like, what?" The manager had heard their conversation, and came from the back to the front. And he saw the officer, and said no charge to the cashier and the cashier understood. They then came outside the pizza shop. And the officer saw a car parked in front. And he stood near, and placed the paper plate on top of the hood. Feng looking at him eat asked," That not your car, is it?" Lloyd finishing his first slice answered, "It's a habit." And he saw his partner from a distance walking over says, "You be careful working there. From the other lead guy being stab, to your boss doesn't look good, alright?" Feng nodded yes, looking around. And the officer had wiped the grease from his hands, to the pants. And he then reaches into his back pocket, handing Feng a card, with his contact information on it.

Feng looks at the number and thought on the comment. And his partner then stood in front of them, ready to talk with Lloyd. Hill said, "Collazo, and the other cops are taking care of the matter. We better go and patrol, how's the pizza?" Lloyd using sarcasm replies," It could be better, and where are your manners... You see I'm talking here!" Feng then walks away laughing at the remark. Hill then held the plate, and begins to eat the last slice. Lloyd saw, and smirked finishing the bottle water. And he knew Hill had a question in mind, so he waited. Hill then asked," Did you get any info on the guy you were just talking to?" Lloyd answered, "He doesn't know anything, so we question his boss." And they started to walk back to the patrol car, conversating about the man that shot Greg.

Richie that night was at his apartment with the news on. And he sat on the couch, on the phone with Steve in regards to Robbie. Richie watching the news says, "Robbie called and told me about 5 minutes ago. He claimed, had killed a man saying he was wanted man... But, according to the news the guy lived... And the guy attacked him from my understanding." Steve then became frustrated with the whole situation asking, "Where?" Richie then got up, and walked into the kitchen answers, "Around that same club, again... It's on the news right now, the guy lived... This is the second time he got attacked... What do you want to do?" Steve reply,' I told him to stay hidden... You take care of it for good.' Richie now looking at the kitchen table sadly said," Alright." Steve then hung up.

Robbie later that night was asleep at his girlfriend's apartment. And he then woke up to loud knocking at the door. And he began to rub his eyes frowning. And he removed the covers watching his girlfriend sleep. Robbie had got up in his boxers, still hearing the knocking again. And he thought to himself at this hour, it's probably one of the crew members. He then left the bedroom, and shows up at the apartment door to open. He now opened, and saw Richie stand still, smirking at him. And he becoming unmerciful, had reach behind his waist, having him now at gun point. Robbie confused loudly asks," WHAT IS THIS?" Richie now fired two shots to the heart, and saw him break the glass table dead. And when he saw that he was dead, he left.

And his girlfriend named Lisa, had Immediately woke up hearing the shots fired. And she became scared, and rushed out of the bed, looking at the door. And she was in a white night gown, worried that she wasn't alone, softly saying, "Robbie?... Babe?" And she waited for a few minutes, putting on a robe, near her bedside on the ground. And she heard nothing, but complete silence, walking slowly to the door. And she quickly opened it and saw nothing. And she curiously walked the hallway, into the living room and saw him dead. And the door was left opened. And she screams out load, rushing to him overreacting. And she had cried and yelled out for help, gently touching his head cut by the glass. And the couple next door heard and rushed over, seeing her hold Robbie in her arms. And they called the police.

Greg the next morning, was on the resting bed at the hospital watching the news. And the news shown a wanted man named, Robbie Wong. And he recognized him, hearing that he was found dead at his girlfriend's apartment. And he was left clueless, not knowing why. Grey at the time, with his phone near, had called for his assistant to start earlier than expected. Melissa the assistant had agreed, and started that morning.

And at that same time in Lewis's office. Hill, Lloyd and Lugo stood near the desk, trying to figure everything out with the evidence provided. Lewis seated at his desk had gazed at Lugo asking, "So, no trace of Steve Liang?" Lugo thought the comment was rather odd answered," No, I thought the other detectives were watching him?" Lewis looking away disappointed replied," They lost him... Steve probably knew what was up... Also, Detective, you had been watching this man. Even before being put on this case... So, I thought you knew." Lugo then shook his head no, and said, "We need to get ahold of the footage at the shop... Kirk was killed there, not in the woods." Lewis looking at Hill and Lloyd says, "You two go down there and check the cameras... Peter and Mary will meet you there." Lloyd then glanced at the detective asking, "Lugo, what's the owner's name?... Also, what does he or she drive?" He answers, "Richie, the owner drives a green Japanese sports car. I..." Lewis then interrupts saying, "Also!... Officer Collazo, and his partner had the cameras checked around the shooting near Jades club. And the guy they saw was killed this morning, and on the news."

Lugo reply," I saw... I believe, Steve had him killed was what happen... No one else could get close to this kid but him... As for his girlfriend... I'm guessing she wasn't around him at the time... Any news on Roy?" Lewis answers, "We are holding Roy for now. Concerning Robbie's death, we need proof before anything detective... Lisa, his girlfriend, is too scared to talk right now. I assigned Peter with Mary to question the owner of Jades... Let's finish this case gentlemen."

They all got up. And Hill and Lloyd left the office first. And the sergeant watching Lugo, walk close to the door quickly asked," Detective, tell me something?" He stopped and turned his attention to Lewis. And he says," Terry, told me that you were with Steve and Richie... Right?" Lugo knew where he was coming from answered, "Yes sir." And the sergeant, with a disappointed look on his face asked," Why didn't you arrest him?" Lugo answered," We need to know where their source of money comes from, boss... Steve's house alone, would indeed make him a millionaire." Lewis thought on the comment says," I can fire you for this, Detective... Don't let it happen again!" Lugo sadly understood said," I won't sir." Lugo then leaves the office feeling awkward, closing the door. And he walked the halls, feeling pressure to finish the case for good.

Alex later that day was at work. And he was an inventory clerk for a warehouse. And he was moving the old product up front, and the newer product to the back. And his boss named Larance, saw him surrounded by boxes at the beginning of the aisle. And his character made him a selfish boss. And he didn't care for Alex because he felt challenged. Larance then came over, and questioned when he would be finished. And he was already frustrated with the inventory, so he answers, "Boss, I started a half an hour ago." And he saw his coworkers, and noticed the boss had provided them with help. And he saw a team of two people in different aisles leaving him without. So, he quickly asks, "Hey!... How come I don't have help?" Larance began to roll his eyes at him. And he then saw a coworker opening the door from the lunch area, coming into the warehouse. And he called the coworker's name shouting, "MARK!... HELP MISTER NEEDY OVER HERE, PLEASE!" Larance continues on to say," Why is it that you always need help, Alex?" And Alex not liking the comment answers, "No, I don't... You want me to do a whole aisle by myself, and I don't understand why... And this isn't the first time either!" Larance frowned and says, "You know I am short staff!... And if you don't like it here, well. ...." Alex, ignoring the remark, had seen Mark come. And to himself, he softly says," I am really tired of this." And his boss overhearing him, standing six feet away, in a mean manner says, "Watch where you're going, Alex!... Thanks, Mark." Mark then bends overreaching for a small box. And their boss had left for the lunch area. And he stood up straight, putting the newer box in the empty slot asking, "Why do you put up with him, Alex?" Alex now saw his coworkers watch, and gossip about him. And he begins to look down, still frustrated with thoughts about leaving the job.

Feng in that same hour, parked in front of a corner store with a bottle of water. And he was talking with Angel. And their conversation was about him quitting his job. Angel asks, "So, what are you gonna do?" Feng seeing a sport car passing by them, answers, "I was talking to my father about IT courses... I'm going do it, man." Angel, then thought of Lloyd asked, "What's the deal with this Lloyd Cop, bro?... He seems fond of you." Feng had taken a sip of water, and smirked at the comment answers, "He feels, he owes me one for saving his life... Also, we went to school together." And he then remembered, his father had wanted him. And he starts to search around for his phone. And Angel watching him in search of something inside the car, had moved aside and asks, "You lose something?" Feng answers, "My father called me an hour ago! Where is my phone, bro?" Angel by chance, looked at the hood of the car, and saw the phone answered, "It's on the hood, bro. "Feng with the phone had called his father, but got no answer. And Angel had laughed and said, "It's Sunday, he probably in church... You do know which church, right?" Feng reaching for the key said, "Yeah, I got to go bro." He then left headed to the church his father usually goes to, which was Army of Elohim.

Feng had arrived at the church and came inside. And he had closed the door seeing his father seated on a purple throne chair, to the right of the pulpit. And his father had seen him near the usher, and glanced at his watch. And he again looked at his father, and saw him tapping the watch a few times. And the bishop of the church was named, "Bishop Luke Meyers." And he at the time, was baptizing the members in a pool with only ten in line. And two ushers with towels had stood near the pool as helpers. Feng then sat down in the back roll waiting for the service to end.

38 minutes later the benediction was given, and the congregation had left. Feng then walked over, and met with his father talking with the bishop near the steps of the pulpit. Lo then introduced him saying, "This is my son, Feng... Remember?" Bishop Meyers remembered, and greets him says, "Yes, yes indeed I do... Feng, your father finally said yes to joining the church." Feng was happy, but curious asking, "Dad, was this why?" And his father had smiled, answers, "I told your mother not to say anything." And he wonders where she was, immediately felt a hug from behind. Now, Polly in a purple elegant dress had release him says, "It's me, Feng." And he then faced her and admired her dress. And they all smelled the sweet perfume she wore. And the bishop amazed at the family says, "Wow!... The whole family is here." And they all laugh at the remark. And they now saw a deacon come over from the bishop's office, with a towel for him. And the bishop saw and received a towel, watching the ushers cover the pool said," Thank, you."

The Feng's then waved the bishop goodbye leaving church. And the bishop then went with the deacon to his office to change clothes. The Feng's then came outside the church conversating about what's for lunch. And their son wanting to surprise them, interrupts by saying, "Tomorrow is my last day at the club." And they were filled with joy over his decision. Polly said, "You can do better, son... Ever thought of working fulltime in ministry like your father?" Feng replies, "No... I want to do IT work... I must go to college first." And he with a question in mind had asked, "What are you going to teach, pop?" Lo answers, "Many things, son... Like the ways of God... What different angels do, their names and what the color of their wings mean... You remember I told you about the archangel Uriel dealing with prophecy and keeping records. Angel's original height is massive and not like a man's height... And if they are our height, it means that they feel sorry for you... And that your level is too low... Less not forget, if the worship music gets cut off too soon, they cry... And they love the book of Hebrews... I will teach the church all these things, and the word of God." And his mother says, "You remember when you were ten, you heard celestial singing in your room?... Those were Angel's son." And he reply, "I remembered, I couldn't sleep those nights... Thanks for reminding me, mom." And they all laugh at the remark looking both ways and cross the street to their cars. And they headed home for lunch.

Now, it became evening time and the officers had arrived at the mechanic shop. And they had parked in front looking at the building. Lloyd getting out the patrol car said, "I bet you we will find something, Hill." Hill shutting his door replies," If not, you're buying me lunch." And they had seen the auto repair door open, with two mechanics working under a car. And their names were Larry and Mick.

Mick saw them enter and looked at their uniforms. And out of curiosity, he got up and asks, "Officers, can I help you?" Hill looks around and asks, "Where is your boss? We have a warrant, for an arrest for a Steve Liang... We were told he comes here on the regular... Is Steve here, or maybe the owner?" Larry then got up, wiping his hands with a rag answers, "The owner went out for a lunch break... And I haven't heard of this Steve Liang guy!" Larry then questioned Mick walking around the battery area said," Mick!" Mick looking at the cops, answered," Yeah! What's up?" Larry asks, "Have you heard of a regular customer called, Steve Liang?" Mick thought on the comment answers, "No... Not at all, you said a regular, right?... No." And he continues working, without a care. Larry asks, "Officers, are you sure you came to the right place?" Lloyd gazed at the mechanic, and his partner about to work under the car again. And he asked, "Where your surveillance room?" Larry then walked with him to the office.

And his partner stayed with Mick working, waiting for the boss to show up. And he receives a vibrated text message. And he checked, and saw it was Peter. And he had said to himself, in an impressive manner," They're here."

Chapter 5

Larry then opened the door, and pointed to the video surveillance system to the left of the desk. And the officer stood near the door, looking at a 50-inch screen asking, "Do you know how far back the system goes?" The mechanic shrugs and answers, "Maybe a month, I don't know... The boss should be back anytime now." Lloyd wanting to know how it works asks, "You know how to work the settings?" Larry, standing by the door, had come over to check it out. And he replies, "It shouldn't be hard at all... What are you looking for?" Lloyd frowning at the remark, answered, "It's police business."

Now, around that time. Richie shown up, and saw something was off. And he driving slowly, saw a cop car parked next to a car in front. And he got nervous, and drove away. And he had thought to himself, that this is not good. And he called Steve, worried that they're after him too. Steve answers, "Yeah." Richie with haste, says, "Listen, the cops are parked in front of my mechanic shop... I don't know,man !... What do you think?" Steve asked, "Are they getting something fix or you don't know?" Richie driving fast around the block answered, "I don't know." Steve, given the situation some thought says, "Call one of your workers, and ask what do the cops want.... It could be nothing." Steve then hung up. And he thought about the comment hanging up too .

Hill at the time, had walked around looking at the camera angle. And he, becoming curious about the boss asks, "Tell me a little bit about your boss, what's he like?" Mick then got up from under the car. And he wipes his hands, using a towel from the ground answering, "He's easy going, I guess... I only been working here for two weeks." And the officer looks at the customer service desk near the office. And he saw no one there, so he asked," How come there's no one at the customer service desk ?" Mick in a sarcastic manner answered," This late, Larry handles it... And the boss if present." And the officer nodded at the comment, still looking around.

Richie eight minutes later, had stopped at a stop light on red calling the office. And in his office the mechanic saw Richie's number, and ignored the call. And Lloyd thought it was odd of the mechanic to not answer, asks, "Aren't you guys still open?" Larry smirking at the comment answered, "We'll be behind, like I am helping you right now." And Lloyd ignored the remark and viewed the footage. And the other detectives had entered the office. And the officer saw, and continued to watch.

Richie at the time was waiting for an employee to answer. And he heard a motorcycle from behind and had glanced at the rear-view mirror. And he saw it was one of the members of Powers named Ed, wearing their signature vest with a helmet. And he was the right-hand man in Powers. And he loved to instigate, and was a kiss up to the boss. And he, being behind him, was waiting for the light to turn green. Richie, recognizing who it was, had turned around making eye contact. And he quickly begins to look for a gun in the glove compartment. And the biker then reached for a gun from behind the waist, and starts to shoot at his head. And Richie immediately leaned down, and starts to speed. And he almost hits a car turning left. And he starting to have anxiety, heard horns sounding from behind.

And the biker had decided to let's him go due to the red light, and cars speeding. And Richie had hung up, and continued to speed leaning up. And he began to panic looking back, but doesn't see Ed. And he approaches another stop light on red, and stopped. And he quickly reaches for the gun again, and sees it's hidden, underneath a manual book loaded. And he saw the light had turned green, and entered into another city line. And he held the gun while entering a 24 hour diner parking lot.

And he calls Steve again, and tells him about the attack that just happened. And outta anger he says, "Ed almost killed me, boss!... We all see each other here and there... But, next time it's on!" Steve reply, "They want revenge for Kirk... Did you find out what the cops wanted?" Richie calming down answers, "Nobody picked up... I'll be there tomorrow morning." Now, Steve, thinking the whole situation was odd says, "If its trouble, don't go back... How's everything else?" Richie looking over his should answers," Things are ok, but... Question, why not sell drugs like we use to boss? And yes, we do get a percentage from the gas... But, why not." Steve then paused and answers, "All the gangs in the city including us made that mistake. And our area got hot with the police... Selling drugs was my brother's idea... You knew, he sold it in the area Powers controlled... Along with the sexual affair which is why they're against us... Where going into human trafficking. I'll leave our gas operation the way it is, and won't open a business... I have a big investor overseas... You're the only one that knows where to find me. I tell you, and you tell the crew what I want done... If you need me, you know where to find me." And he heard him hang up. And he takes a breather watching people go in and out the dinner. And after a while, he became relaxed, and fell asleep.

Ed had driven to a bar in West Haven. And the bar had a lot of people, among the members. And the members were wearing their leather vests with the word Powers written on it. Ed then arrived, and went inside. And he wanted to tell the biker Lord, about who he had seen. And the biker Lord named Vin, was with his girlfriend Wendy. And he was a very direct, and conniving person, which made him the leader. And he would use his size and height to intimidate people. And his girlfriend's character was caring and insecure. And she was in love with him, despite his behavior towards her and others. And the couple at the time, was seated drinking beer. And he met with Vin asking, "Can I talk to you in private?" Vin then glanced at him and got up. And they walked outside to the entry door, and saw no one present. And the biker lord, with his hands in the pocket had asked, "What's up?" Ed smirked and answers, "I ran into one of Steve's boys tonight... Richie!... I had fired at him, but he drove off at a red light... Steve, must still be around hiding." Vin then stared at Ed, asking, "So, you didn't kill him?" Ed looks around, and seeing no one answered,"No." Now, Vin with a serious look in a mild manner says, "He took Kirk out!... So, we'll take one of his boys out too... You see him again, you kill him!... Understand!" Ed answered, "Yes, sir." And they went back inside.

Now, later in the evening at Jades. Feng had showed up at Greg's door knocking. And he was ready to talk to Melissa the Ast. Manager about him quitting. And she was at the desk watching the cameras. And she heard and says, "Come in." And he walked in the office closing the door. And he saw a curly blonde woman, reviewing reports on the desk asked, "You have a minute?" Melissa then looked at him replies," Yeah, What's up?" He then came and stood at the desk, and says ,"I was waiting for Greg to come back to tell him this... I quit." Melissa, giving her full attention, was caught off guard. And she paused for a few seconds, and says,

"Greg is not here, but we must honor your decision... Are you sure you want to quit?" Feng had nodded yes. And she leaned back, and thought about who she could replace him with. And she still in thought says," Alright, I will tell Greg... You take care, Feng... And I apologize for not having a meeting with you all... I'm playing catch up." Feng smiled and walked away. And he opened and close the door behind him. And he remembers the advice Lloyd had given him. And he reached into his wallet, and found his contact card. And the officer at the time, was seated on the couch in the living room. And he heard his phone go off. And he answered, "Hello?" Feng reply, "It's Feng." Lloyd remembering him, answers, "Oh, hey man!... What's up?" Feng replies, "I took your advice, bro. .... I don't work at the club no more." Lloyd chuckled at the comment and reply, "Good for you." And they continued talking for a good 20 minutes. And he then left shortly after, heading home for the evening.

The next morning at the Police department on the stairway. Lugo and Lewis were gossiping about Steve Liang. And the sergeant holding his cup of coffee asks, "So, you haven't seen this man at all is what you're saying?" And the detective, with an attitude, answers ," Because you guys move too fast, and got Roy... Steve, trusts Richie to give orders until he feels safe to appear again. And with a warrant out for his arrest... You tell me, boss!" Lewis begins to frown, not liking the attitude. And he given it back says," You watch it, Lugo!... This wouldn't had happened, had you arrested him like you were supposed to!"

Lewis continues to say," Also, according to the evidence from the footage... Steve killed Kirk. Listen, when you see Richie, you turn him in too." Lugo quickly answers," You'll be making a big mistake if you arrest him now... You want Steve to come out, right?" Lewis then understood where he was coming from says, "I see. You see Steve, you tell us... I am trying to avoid giving you a few days, Lugo... I am headed, to go over a few things with Monty now." Lugo knowing two Monty's, curiously asked, "The Chief of Police, Monty?" Lewis nodded yes. And the detective, now in thought of powers says, "I'm surprise, that powers hasn't taken revenge for kirk already." And the sergeant starts to walk downstairs saying, "Focus on finding Steve, Detective." He then frowned at the remark, and received a text from Chi. And when he opened it, the text read, Where are you?... Come to the wine store and look out now! Lugo then texted back he was on his way and left.

20 minutes later, he arrived parking in front of the busy wine store. Chi then met with Lugo, as he rolled down the passenger side window, saying," Just stay out here, and watch for anything... Meaning the cops, alright?" Lugo nodded yes, and had a question. So, he asked," Why here, why a wine store?" Chi laughed and answered," Crowds... It's a busy store and area. "

Terry at the time had parked near and across watching. And he heard Chi say," To answer your question, you will be making real champion chip money soon. You gotta prove yourself worthy first, right?... I remember last year, we made 2 million pushing drugs with Mr. Smith... But, Steve doesn't want it anymore, he never pushed drugs... His interest is in the gas business, because it's more profitable... Our orders are to check the gas stations on Paris, and Lewy Ave out of money. Jimmy on Paris ave, a former member thought he could cut ties with us... He found out different." Lugo, out of curiosity about the other owner had asked," So, the owner on Lewy isn't a member then?" Chi then shook his head no and says," No, Tommy isn't. We made him an opportunity before... Be on the lookout, Lugo." Chi then received a phone call, so he walked away. And the detective had come out the car, speaking to the wire said," Terry, please tell me you heard that?" And he laughing, replied," Yes, I heard." And he called Lewis for a police watch regarding the gas stations. And he continued to watch Lugo until he was released.

Nia and Alex around that time, were home arguing in the living room. And the argument had to do with Alex quitting his job. And he becomes upset that she was really on him shouts, "WHY DON'T YOU GO BACK TO NEW JERSEY!" And she out of angry, answers in a loud manner, "HOW COULD YOU SAY THAT TO ME!... I AM NOT DEALING WITH DAD'S ABUSIVENESS AGAIN!" And he ignores her, and was followed into the kitchen asked, "Why didn't you report your boss, or at least look for a job before quitting?" He then stood to the table, with his back turned away from her... And she showing great concern, now says," What are we supposed to do now!... I can't cover the whole rent alone, Alex!" He then pushes the table over out of frustration, and faced her shouting, "I WILL FIND A JOB!... I JUST WANT YOU OUT OF MY LIFE !" And it became quiet for a few seconds. And her feelings had gotten hurt by the comment. And he then relies what he had done, and begins to walk towards her. And she, with tears streaming down her eyes, had avoided him. And she ran upstairs to her room, and slammed the door shut. And he shouts, "NIA! I DIDNT MEAN IT !... NIA!" And she had cried lying in bed, and after some time had passed fell asleep. And her brother sat on the couch, making some quick decisions.

It then became 10:45 am, and Richie had woken up rubbing his eyes. And he then glanced at his watch and saw the time. He was still parked in the diner lot and saw a few cars around. And he then got himself together, and called the customer service desk.

And one of the mechanics heard the phone ringing, and ran to the desk to answer. And Richie recognized the voice saying ,"hello?... Adam?" Adam the supervisor, knowing who it was reply," Richie, boss?" Richie quickly replies, "Yes, it's me... Listen, what did the cops want last night?" Adam was reaching for a clean towel at the desk confuses answered, "I wasn't working last night, so let me ask?" And he then yells to Larry, wiping the grease from his hands about last night? And Larry answered, "Checking the security cameras, and took footage... Two detectives also showed up, wanting to talk to the boss was all !"And Adam thought the situation was odd answered," They came to check the cameras, and wanted to talk to you... Boss, is everything alright?" Richie removes the phone from his ear, and starts thinking on the whole situation. He then remembers what Steve had told him to do. And he says to himself, someone must have told, but who?... I should have turned the cameras off that day. Richie fearfully continues with the thought being if Steve ever found out, he would kill him. But, if the cops saw everything .... Then why no warrant for my arrest? And Adam not hearing anything asked, "... Boss?... Are you there?" He heard Adam and answers, "Yeah... Let me talk to who worked last night." Adam had called Larry over. And he came over and answer the phone saying, "Yeah." Richie then asks," What happen, and did they take anything?" He answered, "They wanted to check the cameras out, and talk with you... And they did take the footage for Police business... I help the officer out... Why, am I in any trouble?... I believe they had a warrant... And the officer with me, had spoken about some guy name Steve being seen here... Who's Steve?... And how could I forget !... When asked about Garcia, as they checked the roster and schedule... I had pointed them out to her phone charger in your office... She had left her pink charger, plugged to the wall near your desk." Richie then got out of the car, kicking it out of anger. And he remembered, that she would always charge her phone in his office. And he stressing out, loudly asked," AND THEY WANTED TO TALK WITH ME?"

Larry feeling put in a corner answers ," Yeah... They might come again to see you." And he, calming down now says, "Alright...

Also, your fired!" Larry with a puzzle look said, "What?" Richie then hung up, and threw the phone inside the car. And he was left with the thought being I can't go to the cops, because that's what they want. Steve will find out one way or another... What if I turn him in? Richie was now pacing around his car. And customers were going in and out watching him.

And the manager then came out of the restaurant, and stood sincerely looking at him across the street. And the manager then met with a cop car pulling up in front. And he was now filing a complaint against Richie. So, he complained about him not being a customer, and was parked all morning long. Richie saw, and went inside his car and drove off. And the manager saw, and began to shout at him for leaving. And the officer saw it, and thought it was funny.

Larry at the time, had gathered his things from the locker, and came outside with Adam. And they talk about the firing for a moment. And Larry was the type of guy, that always gave his all. So, the firing came as a shocker to him.

Steve then drove near, wearing shades with a young lady named Mia. And he sent her to gather information on Richie. And she came, and met with them asking," Hey... Is my boyfriend Richie here?" Adam said," Be right with you." He then looked at Larry and says, "Again. I am sorry, Larry." And he, upset, had walked away with his head down to his truck, and drove off. And he then gave his full attention answering," Richie, isn't here... Sorry." Mia immediately asks, "The cops do anything crazy to him?" Adam thought the comment was strange, replies," Richie had spoken with you about the cop's situation, I see." Mia then lied about her name says," I'm Becky by the way, and yes." They then shook hands. And she says, "I came down here because I was worried... He's not answering any of my messages... What did they want?" Adam had smirked, looking at her slim body out of lust answers," The cops took some footage was all... Nothing had happened with Richie, to answer your question." Mia in a worried state asks," Footage?" Adam nodded yes, and saw her look back at the car. And she begun to walk back to the car saying," Thank you, I'll find him." And they drove off in search for Richie that morning.

Feng later that day, was leaving a clothing store empty handed. And he at the time, was in the shopping plaza in East Haven. And Tylor, his former coworker had driven in and parked. And he came out the car, with the pizza shop on his mind. And he glanced around, and saw Feng from a distance. And he, still upset with Feng, had decided to approach him to make trouble. And Feng was walking to his car looking down, and heard his name being called. And he looked up, and saw Tylor meeting him by his car. And he heard, and saw the motorcycles coming into the plaza. And he met with Tylor asking, "Tylor... What's up?" And Tylor out of frustration replies, "I can't find a job! I had a good job... And you got my fired, man!" And he glanced at the car with a devilish grin, and had pointed asking ,"Is this your car?" Vin at the time with ten members, had parked in front of the pizza shop. Tylor, hearing him answer yes, immediately starts kicking the car a few times. And he caused a dint on the passenger side, being told off by Feng. And he then reached into his pocket for a key to scratch the car. And Ed gets Vin's attention to the situation that was across from them.

Feng out of shock, shouts out, "I DON'T OWE YOU ANYTHING, MAN!... ARE YOU CRAZY?" Feng then punched him with a quick blow to the stomach. Powers amazed, had watch Tylor bent over dropping a key. And Feng taking full advantage, had knocked him out with a quick punch to the face. And he was now lay out on the ground, near a customer's car. And Feng upset, had dragged his body, and sat him on the sidewalk. And he looked around and headed back to his car. And he stared at the dint reaching for his keys. And Powers had applauses Feng, and it got his attention. And he, not wanting to be noticed, had left. And Vin watching him leave, glanced at Ed and said, "Best action I've seen all day, Ed." And Ed had nodded with a smirk. And they came crowding the pizza shop.

Now, Feng was headed to see his girlfriend, and immediately received a call from Polly. And he saw the number and picked up. And she, in a worried manner reply, "Hello, Feng?" He then stopped at a red-light answers, "Yeah. What's up?" And she with anxiety quickly yells, "FENG! FENG!... IT'S YOUR FATHER!... WERE HEADED TO THE LUX HOSPITAL RIGHT NOW!" And he began to panic as the light turned green. And he makes a left turn saying," I'm on my way right now!" And he, being focused on a quicker route, had thrown his phone at the passenger seat. And he immediately receives a call from Nia. But he paid no attention, because it was left to silent mode.

10 minutes later Feng had arrived at the hospital. And he immediately saw Nia from a distance, waiting for him at the entry door. And he was caught off guard, closing the car door. And he met with her asking, "How'd you know I'd be here?" And she replies, "I call you, and you didn't pick up... So, I called your mother, and she answered."

And they came inside, and checked in asking for his father. And the nurse, hearing him out, then understood who he was. And she told them to take a seat in the waiting room. And she also said that the ER and the assistant were with his father. And she says I believe he also has company too. And he, becoming confused asked," Company?... What company? "Nia then reached for his hand, and pulled him into the waiting room.

And the deacons and Polly, at the time were standing outside the room hoping everything goes well. And she not seen her son, begun to wonder where he was. And she walked down the hall to the front desk. And she glanced in the waiting room, and saw them. And they saw and met with her. And Feng worried asks, "Mom, what happen?" And she in concern answers, "We were getting ready to go out to dinner... And he went to look for his keys, and couldn't stop coughing... And he couldn't breathe, and fell out in the living room." Nia in concern, had joined hand with her says," Oh my goodness. Is he sick or ...?" Feng hearing footsteps answered, "It's lung cancer." And the deacons then came into the room, and greeted them. Now, the entrance door had opened, and everyones attention was caught.

Ken Feng and his wife Susan had entered the hospital. Along with her older sister named, Narly. And her sister's character made her wise, and caring. And they all saw them in the waiting room. And they had never met Nia before, had greeted her. And Mrs. Feng was still worried about her husband. And Feng saw, and comforted his mother with a hug. And he says, "He is going to be alright, mom.... Did you tell the bishop?" She calms down and answers, "Thank you, I needed to hear that... Twenty-two years we've been married... No, everything happened so fast." And he said, "Come, let's take a seat."

And they sat down in their thoughts. And he not seeing Michelle, had asked," Ken?... Where's Michelle?" Ken answered," She's outta state with a friend." Feng then nodded, and continued to comfort his mother. And Ken, Susan and Narly stayed for two hours then left.

Feng, Nia, Polly and the deacons waited all night. And they fell asleep into the next morning. And It became 2:43 a.m, and a nurse came to wake everyone up. And the nurse said, "The doctor said we're going to have to keep him... And that you all should go home, and get some rest." And the nurse then left. And they got up worried, and ready to leave. And the deacons had told Polly, that they won't stop praying for the family and left. Everyone that morning, had Lo on their mind.

And in that same morning at Richie's apartment, he had received a phone call from Steve in bed. And he, looking at the number, had taken a deep breather. And he answered," Yes?" Now, Steve, in a calmly mannered voice ask ," What did the cops want?" Richie then sits up and answers, "They wanted to get their lights fix, nothing more." Steve asks, So, why didn't you call me back. Why did I have to call you?... You're not lying about anything, are you?" Richie quickly replied, "NO! .... I do everything you ask me!... I'm sorry I didn't call you back. I have been busy with the shop... What's the next order, boss?" Steve replies, "Be on your guard if anything... It's too early for me to host a meeting with everyone. You are my eyes, remember." Richie, with a question in mind asks, "Do you think Powers wants revenge?" Steve laughed and replied, "Most likely.... You are my eyes, Richie... Now, what do you know about Lugo?" Richie had scratched his head with a confused expression speaking up. And they spoke about Lugo for a good 10 minutes. And he then, was given more orders to carry out.

And in that same hour at the Feng residents. Feng and Nia were arguing in the living room, about him not working. Polly at the time, was in the kitchen washing dishes, having thoughts of Lo. And he loudly says, "WHY HERE? WHY HERE, NIA?" She arguably replied, "Alex quit his job, now you?... I apologize if you're taking this too hard, Feng!... But, do you see a future with me?" Feng avoiding her, had looked to the window answers," You know I love you... Why do you want to fight?" She then became curious regarding his actions asks, "Did you think about me before quitting?... What if we had a family?" Polly had heard enough, and began to frown. And she then turned the sink off, and met with them shouting," ENOUGH! PLEASE!" Feng then walked away into the kitchen saying, "I'm so tired of this!" And she saw, and in a sarcastic manner replies, "Well walk away then." Polly then focused on her asking, "Why are you being mean to him?" Nia never having confrontation with her answers, "I apologize if you think I am... We spoke of having a future together, and it scares me when he quits a job like that." And she, given it some thought, curiously asks, "Was it for something better?"

Nia looking down, immediately has a flashback of her childhood days. She remembered her father's gambling addiction, and him not keeping a job, costing them their home. And they were homeless for six months. And she never shared this, and didn't want to relive it again. Nia then snaps out of it, said, "I didn't ask him." Polly in concern says, "Start asking questions before jumping at him, ok?... Ever asked yourself how he may feel?... If you want a future with him, learn how to talk to him." She then understood, and went into the kitchen for Feng. And she saw him seated avoiding her, eating an apple facing the window. And she met with him saying," Feng!... I'm sorry!" And he continued to look at the window, ignoring her. She then sat on his lap, and tried to take a bite of the apple to gain attention. And he laughs at her saying, "You crack me up." And she laughed back, glancing at Polly. And Polly saw them from the living room, and smiled at them. And she said to herself, communication is the key to a great relationship. And they spent the rest of the day, comforting Polly.

Two days later, Lo had recovered being well rested in the hospital. And Polly was called to take him home, and to let him rest. And when Lo came home, he couldn't wait to give his testimony leading to Sunday. And he shared with the family, that he saw the lord's finger in a vision pointing at him, and it healed him. And the family was amazed and happy with the testimony.

Sunday then came. And the Feng's, Nia and the deacons were ready for service at Army of Elohim. And Paster Lo Feng had stood up from his seat at the pulpit, after praise and worship. And he received a round of applause from the church. Now, Bishop Meyers at the pulpit stand had called him to testify. Lo, being given the microphone in a cheerful voice says, "I first want to give honor to God, who is the head of my life!... My wife Polly, and my son Feng... I think God for healing me... I know him as a healer!"

And the church agreed by saying Amen! Lo then turns around, and looks at the bishop now seated behind him says, "Bishop, I don't know what else to say... Other than, God healed me!... God, has no respect of person!... If he did it for me, he'll do it for you!" And the whole entire church got up, and agreed with him. And the church had joy, and some dance around. And he in remembrance said, "Thank you, Jesus!" And he hands over the microphone to the bishop. And the church had cheered for him. And the Bishop with excitement in his voice reply, "Won't He do it! You don't serve a dead God!... Praise the lord!... Paster Lo Feng, I thank you for suring that revelation with us about Moses... Why he didn't make it to the promise land... Pastor took us to 1 Corinthians10:4, and Hebrews too... This was at a bible study a month ago." Lo seated, had nodded to the remark saying," Honoring !... Honoring !"

Nia at the time, had felt a sweet presents all over her, and began to develop tears. And she, having tears of joy, had felt loved. And she then knew, that this was the family she had always wanted. And the bishop looking around the church says," Alright, it's time to worship again saints !" And the church began to worship for 20 minutes, and the bishop preached. And after the church service was done, the Feng family went home to celebrate Lo's healing.

Now, Lo, Feng, Nia and the deacons sat at the kitchen table eating what Polly made. There at the table was turkey, baked potatoes, rice, green peas and ham. Polly then sat down a bowl of gravy saying, "Please, eat up everyone." Bishiri now staring at the bowl says, "What an awesome service, right?" And the other deacons agreed, passing the gravy around for their food. Polly then sat with Lo, and they kissed. And she had glanced around blushing at the kitchen table, knowing the deacons never saw this side of them. Nia saw and admired them said,"Aawww." And she glanced at Feng, and they kissed as well. Polly then became curious about her parents asks, "Nia... Are your parents married?" She then looked down at her plate embarrassed answers, "No... They were together for 8 years, and then divorce... My mother was still in love with her ex, and left us... Dad never remarried". Lo heard her out and was disappointed. And he said, "I am sorry to hear that... Has your family accepted Jesus?" Nia shook her head no answered," No, we haven't."

Nia quickly says," I want the relationship you both have... I mean, you both love each other." Feng now comforting her, looking at the peas says, "Nia, they like you. Shepard... hand me the peas please." Shepard then hands the bowl filled with peas, listening to their conversation. And Polly with another question for Nia, had smiled asking, "How's your brother?" Nia smiled and answered, "Alex is fine... Same with all of my family in New Jersey." And she wanting to change the subject asked ," Why doesn't Feng have siblings?" Lo glanced at his wife now eating replied, "Feng was a blessing sent from heaven. We indeed wanted more children but, he only came." Shepard being sarcastic, said, "Hey!... Maybe Feng might become the next Paster Lo Feng, right?" Feng quickly answered," Don't count yourself out my friend!" They all laugh out loud at the comment. And then after laughter, had enjoyed the food.

Chapter 6

Polly then puts her fork down to the plate, and wipes her mouth with a napkin. And she, now with an idea to bond had asked, "Nia, are you doing anything this afternoon?" She looks at Feng giving no expression, reply, "I don't think we have anything plan." Polly says, "My husband and I are going shopping after this... Would you like to join us?" She quickly answered, "Sure, I'd love to." Lo then stood up, and called Feng by name, and waved him to come follow. Everyone else saw and continued to talk and eat. And he, now opening the back door, stood with Feng in the middle of the backyard says," I didn't expect this big meal today, but... you were on my mind back at the hospital." And Feng had no clue, what he was talking about. And his father reached into his back pocket, and handed him a thick envelope. And Feng opened it and saw a lot of money, not understanding why asks, "Dad? ..." And he knew his son was clueless, answers," It's for your schooling, IT... It's fifty grand... Ok?" He was amazed, and hugged his father. Now, Polly then shows up to the door calling them back. And they saw but needed a moment alone. And Lo, loving his amazed expression said," After you son." And they came back inside and had a good time.

Richie two hours later, had shown up at the shop not knowing what to expect. And he parked in front, looking around. And he was very nerves about leaving his car, and rushed inside. And Adam with Jason at the auto repair area, saw him go into the office. And they wondered, what's was going on. And Adam around the tires, had seen the office door open. And he volunteered to go and question him. And he showed up at the door, and saw Richie seated asks, "Boss, You ok?" Richie glanced at him and answers, "Yes and No... Did these cops come back?" Adam reply, "I haven't seen them, I been covering for you... They must have gotten what they had wanted." And Richie looked up, taken a breather. And he glanced at his security system, knowing he was right. And he says, "If you see the cops, tell me... I have to go and clear my head." Now, Adam knew then, that he was under a lot of stress said, "Alright." Richie then left the office, and drove away. And Detective Peter with Mary five minutes later, had parked in front. And they came, and questioned the mechanics, receiving no answers. And Adam called Richie shortly after, and he never came back. Lewis later told the detectives not to visit anymore. But, watch the shop from a distance. And he was convinced that Lugo would deliver.

The Feng's with Nia that afternoon went shopping in Hamden. And they were in an uncrowded clothing store, checking out everything. Polly with Nia were in the lady's area. And, Feng and Lo were in the men's area surrounded by their bags. And Nia was looking at a purple shirt, with diamonds in the middle saying," This shirt is cute... Let's see how much?" Polly saw and answers, "Don't you worry how much it is... We'll buy it for you." Nia, not being used to kind people says, "You guys are good people.... I don't want you to think I am after anything." Polly smiled and replies," Feng hasn't spoken evil of you, Nia... Just treat each other right." And she nodded at the remark, watching the fellas. And the fellas began to hold their bags.

And they now waited for the ladies to finish up. And a female cashier saw, and came from the register to see if they all needed help. And Lo had waved the cashier away, and said to Feng, "Your mother can shop, can't she." Feng laughs at the remark, watching the girls replied," Yes, Indeed... Two hours of shopping, and now I have my boots and stuff.... What did you buy?" Lo answered, "Pants and shoes." And his son looked down at his father's foot size, and laughed. And Lo, not understanding asked," What's funny?... And why are you looking at my feet?" And Feng, calming down form laughter asked, "What size are you, an eight?" Lo answers, "No... Nine and a half... I don't wear a size twelve like you do." And the cashier at the time, had checked on everyone, and came back to the register. And Lo says," Let's get your mother attention so we can go back home... Who's playing tonight?" Feng answered," I have no idea." And within 5 minutes they all came to the register. And Polly paid for everything using a credit card. And they then came out of the store to their SUV, and left .

Six minutes later, Lloyd had drove into the plaza off duty, and parked. And after locking the car door, he went inside the same store. And he thought to himself, all I need is a white button shirt for Vicky tonight. And he goes over to the men's area to look around. And the female cashier saw and came over asking," Can I help you find anything sir?" And before he could answer, walks inside a young, long dark haired, Italian woman dress casual in all black.

And she was beautiful to gaze upon, and her name was Renee De Nino. And she was making her way to the lady's area with her phone, and a small purse. And the cashier at the time, facing him had said sir a few times. And he then snaps out of it, answered, "I'm fine miss." And the cashier had walked back to the register. And he continues to glance here and there at her.

Now, Renee had received a phone call. And after checking the number, she answers, "Hello?... Chi Chi, what do you want?" She then walked around, as the same cashier came to help. And she saw from a distance, and waved her away, looking at a pair of black pants. And she held up the pants and frowned. And she arguably asked, "And you want me to do what?... No! No!... You always do this to me!" Renee then turned around, and made eye contact with Lloyd. And she quickly turned back, avoiding him, and continued to shop. And he thought to himself ,"Maybe one day, now is not the time." And he looked around, and couldn't find the shirt he needed. So, he left the store, not wanting to make her feel awkward.

Lugo and Lewis that same hour was at the police deparment, in the hallway conversing about the case. Lugo says, "Richie is saying Steve was asking questions about me!... What do you think?" Lewis then took a breather and answers, "It could be several things... He doesn't know who to trust but this Richie fellow... The footage shown him shooting the guy and girl. And those seen with him has a warrant also... Maybe he needs another right-hand man for the just in case." Lugo in thought says, "You might be on to something. Say.... You don't think Steve wants me to kill him?" And Lewis, given it some thought replies," Could be... Does, Richie knows who killed Robbie?" Lugo thought about the comment reply, "My guest is Steve killed him, or had him killed." Lewis then remembered what was owed to him said," Also!... Today is pay day for me. Come on, give it up." And the detective had reached for his wallet, not liking he owed had paid him back. And Lewis had received the money, walking away saying, "We'll catch them all... Thanks, detective."

And as the months went by, leading to December, at 42 degrees with very little snow on the ground. These were the events that had happened.

Steve had remained hidden, giving orders to Richie as usual. And Lewis continues to explain to Monti, the Chief of Police, about the continued search for Steve.

Lugo then asked Richie about Robbie's death. And he was told that Robbie was killed by him to keep order. Terry hearing their conversation said," Facts!"

Feng and Nia's relationship at the time grew rocky. And this was due to her not letting go of the abuse she was used to.

Greg had come back to work after taking time off. And his assistant had kept him club informed, while he was absent. And a few days later he'd received a call from Brain. And he had quit over the phone, due to his legs. And this had caught Greg by surprised, and now he was in need of another lead guy.

The police then closed the mechanic shop due to the investigation. And the whole idea of keeping it open, was to catch the crew… But, none of the members, including Richie, had come back.

Adam had been running the shop until the investigation started. And the Garcia family at the time, had made the news for two days straight. And they stood outside the shop wanting justice for Jane. And it was then, that a news reporter spoke about her car being found by the police, parked near a junkyard . And the only thing left in her car, was her phone underneath the passenger seat. Steve's fingerprints were found all over Richie's desk. And Richie's warrant for his arrest had then become televised. Now, Chi and Lucky, were the ones being given orders, from Steve by phone. And the crew that was televised had worn disguises, and found a club to meet for orders.

Powers were always on their guard not knowing what to expect from the police, and Steve's crew that remains unknown. Powers did recognize that Steve, and a few members were on the news with warrants. And Vin among the crew, outside a bar had held a meeting. And he though it be best to let the cops have them. And after hearing him out, they were all in agreeance.

Lugo one sunny afternoon, had stood to the corner of the wine store. And he at the time, was watching for cops with Richie present. And the cops very rarely would pass by, due to it being busy area. And Richie wore a bearded disguise, and was now bald headed. And he was going over a few things with the fellas by the entry door. And the manager was on a short vacation at the time, leaving a young, scared supervisor in charge. And he was avoiding them, at all cost. And he knew that they were up to no good, and were in the way of customers. And he was clueless to who they were, and too scared to call the cops. Terry at the time, was parked near watching.

Now came two women in the neighborhood approaching him. One young, and older coming for drugs. And he saw, and looked away knowing what they wanted. And the young lady asks, "Are you holding?" Lugo, now facing her answered," I don't sell drugs if that's what you mean." And the older lady, stereotyped him by his street clothing appearance says, "You look like you do!... We watched you stand here, for a whole half an hour, from our apartment... Are you sure you're not holding?" Lugo with sarcasm asked," Lady, what if I was a cop? .... Have you seen me from somewhere?" Lugo had continued to tell the ladies off, and saw a cop car coming. And the cops patrolling had seen them from a distance, and the sirens sounded. And the crew heard and watched. And the ladies had run away, to avoid the cops. And he saw, and was left with the two cops now parked in front. And the officers were named Sherman and Bully.

And the police then got out of the car and met with him. Lugo then looks back at the wine store, and sees Richie now watching. And he glanced back at the cops asking, "What's up?" Bully asks, "Son, are you selling drugs?" He replies, "You can check me out,

I am not a drug dealer?" Sherman then viewed the direction the women ran in says, "Those two ladies, we warn them last week... If we caught them with anything, we'd arrest them." Lugo then frowned and says, "You're still making me out to be a drug dealer!" And the comment was counted a disrespect to the officers. Bully then gets in his face saying," Tough guy, I see."

Sherman then pulled Bully aside to calm him down. And he turns around, now seeing the crew slowly approaching. Richie asked, "Hey!... What's going on?" Lugo, now with his arms crossed reply, "This is harassment, bro!" Sherman knew they were being watched. And he immediately walked back to the car, saying, "Have a good day, sir." Bully then walked over to the passenger side, and opened the door. And he sat down closing the door, avoiding an apology. And the detective being sarcastic says, "Hey?... Did you forget to say something?" Bully quickly opens the door with haste. And his partner saw and yells, "BULLY, WHAT ARE YOU DOING?... LET'S GO!" And he then stared at Lugo, and slammed the door back. And they immediately took off to avoid any situation. And Terry had already zoomed in, and got their badges. And he then made a phone call to Lewis. And when he received the news, had spoken with the captain about the issue. And the issue got dealt with immediately .

Richie already curious of the situation, loudly asked, "WELL?" Lugo laughs, and met with him answered, "They think I am a drug dealer." Richie then understood nodded, and says, "Listen, we have a meeting with Steve ."Now, the detectives eyes had opened up in shock, asking, "When?" He smiles and replied, "Soon, is what he said... Now come inside with us, those cops won't come back." And the detective did what he was told, and came inside with the crew.

And that same hour at the Feng residents. Lo and Polly were packing for Miami Florida. And their son was on the phone with

Nia in the living room arguing. And the argument was about her saying he was just like her brother regarding, quitting. And he frowning shouts, "HOW?... HOW? YOU ALWAYS WANT TO FIGHT ABOUT SOMETHING!... YES!... YES, YOU DO IF IT DOESNT GO YOUR WAY!" And they heard the argument going on for the past ten minutes. And she hands Lo a blue shirt with a question regarding Nia. Polly asked, "What do you think of Nia?" Lo, now packing the shirt in the travel backpack answers, "I don't really know her that well.... Why?" She in concern for them says, "They argue too much for me... I feel, well ..." Lo then interrupted asking, "You feel what?... That she's not good enough for him, is what you're trying to say?" And she quickly answers, "I never said that, Lo... I feel there was some abusiveness growing up... I have never seen him so tried, and upset... And I understand she his first girlfriend, but... you know what. Maybe she will change, and get saved." And he nodded, replies," If she wants to be a Feng, she must let go of the abusiveness... Time will tell, right?" She agreed with the comment, with a concern for Feng. And she knew that they were unequally yoked. Now, Feng had hung up, ignoring the negative comments, feeling hungry.

    And he went into the kitchen, opening the refrigerator for something to eat. And the doorbell had rang. And he, being nearby goes to answer it asking, "Who is it?" Angel answered, "It's Angel." Feng then opens, and closed the door, greeting him with a handshake. And he curiously asked, "What are you doin today?" Angel had shrug at the comment and sat down. And he watched Feng reach for a bowl of banana pudding, closing the refrigerator. And he says," I'm not working today... Hey, Greg asked about you?" Feng laugh, reaching for a spoon near the sink replies, "The answer is no... We are going into a new year, and I want something new." Angel then understood, and wondered about his girlfriend asks, "How's things with your lady?" And Feng, having a sour look reply, "You're messing with my good nature." And he waited for him to go into detail, but he doesn't. So, he asked, "So, how's the Feng clan?... The churches must have paid your father good, to had lived in the suburbs for so long." Feng's sour look had become laughter, and he finished the banana pudding answering, "They were interior decorators before the ministry, remember... Were Good, tho... They recently were invited to preach at a church out in Miami Florida... With the deacons of course." Angel becoming curious, about him going asked, "You're not going down, bro?" Feng, putting the bowl into the sink answers, "No... I'mma check out the colleges for IT work, tho."Angel then got up from his seat, and looked at the window. And he saw that it was very sunny outside asks," Feng. .... You want to go to a sports bar, and watch a game?... I know a good spot in North Haven." He agreed by nodding yes. Now, Polly then enters the kitchen for her reading glasses near the vase on the table. And she seeing Angel, had smiled and said, "Hey, Angel!" And he answers, "Hi, Mrs. Feng.... Were about to head out!" And she told them to enjoy themselves, and left the kitchen.

Later that afternoon they arrived, and parked at the sports bar lot. And they took notice of Twenty motorcycles being parked together. And Angel gets out the car, and saw Feng says, "It might be a full house, bro." Feng in agreeance, then locked the car.

And when they entered inside, they saw a lot of customers. And they also saw ten female, and ten male bikers. And the bikers were in their vest, and the word Powers, was written bold and big in purple, at the back. And they were all over the restaurant, leaving an uptight vibe.

Vin was around the pool table, playing pool with a few members. And Feng had glanced at Angel, being unfamiliar with the bikers asks, "Do you see these bikers here all the time?" Angel shook his head no and said," Let get a seat, man." And a waitress then came to them, and gave a table asking," What can I get for you guys?" Angel then orders hot wings with a soda. And he order a cheeseburger with fries, and a soda also. And Vin's righthand man around the pool table, had looked over and saw Feng. And he reminds Vin, about him knocking a guy out. And their leader had gazed at Feng, and laugh saying, "I do remember his face." They then continued playing pool.

And twenty minutes later, the waiter came over with their food. And they were now eating their fries, focusing on the game. And they were also being watched by two pretty young ladies at a table nearby. And their names were Gigi and Holle from Powers. And the ladies then came over and met with them.

Now, Gigi in a flirting manner asks, "Can we seat with you guys or .... ?" Angel in lustful manner quickly reply, "Sure! Sure, you can!" Feng now glanced at the ladies, asking, "What do you want?" Holle then felt an attitude being given asked, "What's your deal?... You don't like women or something?" And he being sarcastic, replies, "Or something!... I got a lady, so!" The ladies had left, losing interest due to the comment made. And he looked at Angel and says, "Listen, those girls are nothing but trouble... Look around, bro." He then looks around, seeing the men from Powers staring at him. And he being in agreeance had said, "I see, your right."

Lloyd and Hill five minutes later, had walked inside off duty, and immediately took notice of everything. Hill looked at Lloyd, in a sarcastic manner says, "Well, you pick this place." And he watched his partner fixed his shirt behind the waist. And his cuffs were in his back pocket. And he also carried a gun from behind the waist, underneath his shirt. And his partner quietly asked," Your off, why bring cuffs." Lloyd in a funny manner, had shrug and answered," It's a habit."

And the ladies of Powers, had watched the fellas with a waiter, be seated across from them. And the waiter then took their order. And the women were blushing, and talked about how handsome they look. And after the waiter had left, one of the older members had gotten up and met with them. And she greeted them with a smile and had asked for their names. Lloyd gave his, and Hill refused due to being married. Now, Hill became curious, about her not introducing herself, asked ,"And what is your name, miss?" She answers, "I apologize, It's Nicky!... You guys want to sit with us?" Becky and La La, members of powers had waved at the same time saying together, "Hi!" And the men of powers notice the attention given, and didn't like it. And they saw the men staring stone cold at them. And Lloyd looking back at Nicky, asks, "Is there a reason the boys are looking at us, Nicky?" She had shrug at remark .

And Angel at the time overheard, and saw her talk with Lloyd. And he had gotten Feng's attention by touching his hand, and couldn't believe it was him again. Feng then watched her give Lloyd the number, and sat back with the girls. And he being sarcastic says, "This guy again, man... You gotta pick a better spot next time, bro."

Now, Wendy, had seen Lloyd leaving the bar. And she, loving what she saw, had walked over, and blew him a kiss. And Ed, leaving the bar with a beer, had seen and went to the pool table where Vin was. And Vin at the time, was waiting for his turn with his pool stick. And Ed had met with him and told. And this left him frowning at her actions, asked, "You sure?" Ed given him a reassurance answered," I wouldn't lie to you, man!" Now, Vin had came over with his pool stick to where the girls were. And the manager at the time, was in a meeting with the cooks in the kitchen.

Now, Vin standing at 6 feet 4, bald with tattoos had stood in front of their table. And he waved to Wendy, seated in the middle to come to him. And the girls knew that the flirty had gotten her into trouble. And they had made room for her to meet with him. Now, Wendy now facing him asked, "What's is it?"

And the customers had watched this man come over, and were scared. And twenty-two of them had left, wanting nothing to do with the violence. And she saw the customers, again asks," What is it?" And he pointed at Lloyd, in all seriousness asking, "Did you blow a kiss to him?" She then looks to the ladies for support. And they all immediately looked down avoiding eye contact. And he asks, "You want to sleep with him, is that it?... Don't lie to me, Wendy!" And she, becoming embarrassed quickly says," You know I love you, Vin!... Why? .... Yes, yes... I did blow a kiss to him." And he, out of disgust, had forcefully poked her shoulder with the pool stick. And he shouts out, "SO, NOW YOU WANT TO BE A HOE!... LIKE, SUSAN!" Lloyd, not liking the disrespect had gotten up from his seat says, "Listen sir... I'm sure she was only playing with me, nothing more." And he had looked at Lloyd, ignoring the remark. And he grabbed her by the hair, and drew her close. And he, now in a wicked manner said, "Don't ever disrespect me again!" Vin then throws her down to the floor.

And the manager leaving the kitchen was in conversation with a cook, and saw customers leaving. And out of curiosity, he came to see why, and saw a woman on the floor. And he loudly asked, "HEY! WHAT'S GOING ON HERE?... AND WHY IS THIS WOMAN ON THE FLOOR?" Vin reacted like he was going to hit the manager, walking away said, "Get out of my face!" Ed then walked over, and smiled at the ladies helping her up. And Wendy immediately went to the ladies' room out of embarrassment, and the ladies had followed. And the manager, out of frustration, had left for his office. And the officer had glanced at Lloyd sitting back down, asked, "What do you want to do, Lloyd?... We can leave it alone or arrest him for what he just did." Lloyd then thought about the whole situation, given no answer.

Feng and Angel had decided to leave to avoid the behavior they just witnessed. And he looks at Angel saying, "I almost was going to call the cops at the big man... You don't treat people like that." And as they were leaving, Lloyd saw and recognized Feng. And he, in a sarcastic manner asks out loud, "YO, FENG!... HOW'S EVERYTHING?" And he turns around, and saw him answered," Where's a cop when you need one." Hill immediately looks down to avoid eye contact. Because he didn't want the men in Powers to suspect them as being police officers. And Lloyd, watching them exit out, had ignored the comment. And he looked at Vin in the pool room. And his partner said, "Lloyd, we are off duty." Lloyd, given it some thought replies, "Feng, is right then." Now, his partner looks around, given it some thought too, says," let's ask her first, Lloyd... If she wants to press charges, ok?" He nodded yes and had a bad feeling, reply, "Hill, call an officer in for the just in case.... I have a bad feeling about this... Just do it." Hill had nodded and said, "Alright." And he got up, and walked to the restroom passing the waiter with their food. And his partner began to call for an officer for back up using his phone. And the waiter came and sat down their food and drinks.

Now, Wendy in the ladies' room, was being comfort by the ladies. And one of the members named Trina says, "You said you love him, Wendy." And she wiping her tears with a tissue answers, "I know, I really do love him. And don't, please ladies... Don't get involved with what just happened... I don't need to report anything to the cops." Now, Trina, in thought of the defender says, "That guy out there, was trying to defend you... You think he will call the cops?" And she quickly answers, "If he does, I won't press any charges on Vin... We have a twelve-year-old son together, you know." Trina in agreenace replies, "I know. I know."

Now, It then became awkwardly quite for a few minutes. And they not hearing any violence, begins to wonder. And she asks, "What's going on out there?... You girls hear anything?" Trina with a few women, had left the restroom to go and see.

And they had met up with Lloyd coming out of the restroom area. And he quickly asks, "Hey, that lady on the floor, is she alright?" Trina had became curious, crossing her arms asking, "Yeah.... Why?" Lloyd then read her body language, and knew they were protecting her. And he, playing it off, replies, "Just asking that's all, excuse me." And he then went back to the restroom. And his partner from a distance, had saw the ladies look around. And went back into the restroom again. And he got up, and went to the restroom to find out what's going on. And his partner was in thought about everything around the sink. And Hill then opened the door, making eye contact with him. And Lloyd says, "She's not going to press charges on him." And his partner closing the door, saw that they were alone asks, "You sure about this?" Lloyd answers, "Her friends body language told everything.... It's her life you know." Hill in agreeance nodded and said, "Your food awaits you." Lloyd answers, "I lost my appetite... Let's get out of here."

And Vin saw them leaving the restroom about to exit out. And he with an urgent behavior, leaves the pool table shouting in a hostile manner, "HEY!... HEY!" And one of the men from Powers immediately stood in front, and stop them with his arms cross.

And the manager saw from his office, and came over to beg Vin to stop. But, Ed blocks him from Vin. Now, Vin holding his pool stick says, "If I catch you, or your friend with my girl... I will kill you!" And the officers were in shock by the comment, and made their move. And the rest of the customers were now leaving. Hill, with a serious stare, had met with him asking,

"Do you know who you're talking to?" Vin with a cocky attitude answered, "Should I?" Now, his partner had pulls out his gun from behind, and aimed it at Vin. And Powers were now showing their guns for Vin's safty. And Hill saw, and immediately showed his badge saying, "Sir!... You have the right to remain silent, turn around!" And he smiled, and in a sarcastic manner says, "You two are pigs?... I had no idea." And he drops the pool stick, and turns around to be cuffed. And Lloyd, watching the crew put their guns away, had thrown the cuffs to his partner. And his partner immediately cuffed him.

Now, Wendy then came out of the restroom with the girls. And she was in awe, walking to the men of Powers asking, "What happen?" And Ed answered, "Vin had threatened two off duty cops... He had no idea, Wendy." And she had gotten upset, and starts to develop tears, shouting, "WHY ARE YOU SO STUPID!" And she walked over to Vin, ready to strike, balling her fists. And Lloyd saw, and blocked her from attacking him. Now, Officer Jazz and Monti had entered in, and saw Vin. And Jazz asked, "Is this him?" Lloyd putting the gun away answered, "Yeah." And the manager wanted nothing to do with the whole situation had walked away. And after everything was explained, they walked him out to the Police car. And Powers, had come out to watch everything. And their leader went inside the police car, and was taken to the Police station.

And the officers looked back at Powers at the entrance, watching the cops leave. And Wendy immediately breaks down, and runs back inside. And the girls had followed her for support. And the officers had begun to walk to Hill's car. Ed and the rest of the crew, had watched them out of dislike, and went back inside. Lloyd then stood around the car says, "I can't stand a man putting his hands on a woman, man!" Hill replies, "Relax Lloyd, ok?... The man got arrested... And it did that bimbo some justice." And his partner gets in, closing the door says," Hill, your right." And Hill, opening the door had faced him reply, "If she never flirted with you, just saying." And he now in remembrance Lloyd's actions loudly says ,"AND, WHAT WAS THAT BACK THERE?... YOU SHOWN NO BADGE!... YOU PULLED A GUN OUT, AND WAS GONNA DO WHAT?" Lloyd gave no answer avoiding eye contact. And his partner got in, and closed the door leaving the area making a left turn. Lloyd given no expression asks, "Did you hear him say the name Susan?" And he calming down now answered, "Yup... I wanna say, there's a lot of cheating going on in that camp." Lloyd asks, "How do you think Powers will operate without their leader?" Hill thought on the comment while driving to his partner's house. And he answers, "It's tough to say... Maybe that lady he's with, will lead them... One thing for sure, if they had any enemies. .... Now is the time to strike." And they arrived at Lloyd's house, and he dropped him off. And Lloyd thought about the whole situation, watching his partner leave. And he reached for his keys in the pocket, and went inside.

  Powers three hours later, came out of the bar, and stood near their bikes in chilly weather. And they were in heavy gossip about Vin being arrested and absent. And Wendy sat on her motorcycle wearing her dark shades giving no answers. And a member named Max was feeling chilly says, "It's almost time to put the bikes away, the weather dropped big time... So, what are we doing in this situation with Vin?" Ed stared at Wendy asking, "How can we then be Powers, Wendy?... We should bail him out so we can continue making drug trades, you know this." And another member named Nicki, had stood next to her saying, "You know he's right." And her tears immediately started to develop, and steamed down her face. And all she wanted was love and peace from Vin. But, she knew that Vin will never change his behavior towards her. And she knew he was needed to lead Powers, and not herself. And she said, "Ed, go and bail him out. I need him, just as well as Powers do." And he smirked at the remark said, "alright. "

Chapter 7

And the next morning at the Feng residents. Polly and Lo were packing their bags in the back seat of the their SUV. And Feng was in bed, waking up at the time. Now, she looks at the back seat, making room for four travel bags. And Polly watched her husband afterwards, move two small bags around, to make room. And he broke a sweat, wiping his face by hand. And he was breathing heavy, due to the weight of the travel bags. And he asks, "Polly, what did you pack love?" And she seeing him take a break, answers, "If you need help, call Feng... And stop complaining!" Now, Lo in thought of Feng asked, "Is he still in bed?" She quickly answered," Of course he is in bed, it's still early." And shortly after he felt energized, he went inside for the bags in the living room.

And he inside, met with Feng in the kitchen. And Feng at the time, was making his way to the refrigerator. And he was stopped by Lo, saying, "Give me a hand, son." And his son had wiped his eyes, and begun to help with the rest of the travel bags. And after they had packed everything up, Polly kissed her son on the cheek. And she, being in a funny manner about his absents says, "Have fun and no sex till marriage, Feng!" And he, now feeling embarrassed, looks away. And he faced her again says, "Seriously, ma!" And she hugged him and got into the SUV. And she about to close the door, was in thought of the deacons, says," Call the deacons, Lo!" And he heard and walked 8 feet away, with Feng. And Lo, now facing Feng says, "I know you will be fine... Listen, if you need us, call us... Any plans?" Feng laugh at the comment and answers, "Sleep for right now... I couldn't sleep last night... I will look around for a college I want to go to... Thanks again." Now, Lo, in thought of Feng's relationship asks, "How's you and Nia?" And Feng begins to scratch his head at the comment replies, "It could be better." And he knew that his father only asked, because he cared. And Lo glanced back at the SUV, and starts to walk back saying, "We'll be back, son. We'll be down there for a while... The deacons want to sing, can you believe that." Feng laughed at the remark and asked," What are you goin to teach out there?" Lo stopped and faced him answers," Mazzaroth, pointing them to Jesus... So, Merry Christmas and Happy New Years, son... And if you change your mind, come with us... Ok?" Feng nodded yes, watching his father get inside the SUV. And he then questioned himself, isn't Mazzaroth the name of a deathly fallen angel? And he watched and waved at them leaving. And then he went inside the house for breakfast, before staring his search.

 Hill and Lloyd three hours later, were assigned to check the parking downtown. And they at the time, had stood around a car, and saw the parking meter was unpaid. Now, Across from them, in that busy area were clothing stores. And Lloyd says, "Put something in the parking meter people... Hill?... Why are we doing this again?" And his partner laughed at what was said, answering, "Lewis wanted us to check this area out, remember... I feel awkward doing this myself."

 And the owner of the car was shopping at the time. And her attention was caught by a lady mentioning cops around a black sports car, across the street. And the woman had recognized the car being her own. And begins to panic, running out of the store. And she met with them asking in a loud voice, "WHAT ARE YOU TWO DOING?... I PAID OFFICERS!" Hill went will the situation, misleading her about giving a ticket says, "You can look at the meter, and tell your time was up two hours ago." And the lady worried said, "Give me a break, officer!... Please!" Hill with a smirk, had walked away says, "Pay the ticket then." Now, The lady looked for the ticket and didn't see anything. So, She quickly got in the car and drove off. And the officers saw, and began to walk to the patrol car.

Lloyd had chuckled at her actions, says," That lady should count her blessings, right?" Hill gave no answer looking around. And his partner had laughed at his mood asking, "Are you, ok?... You seem moody, bro." Hill had ignored the comment, and was ready to open the door to relax.

Now, Wendy at the time, was driving in search of the officers that had arrested Vin. And she had found them in conversation around the patrol car. And she saw a parking space near, and had parked. And she opened, and closed her door, looking both ways ready to cross. And Hill, was opening the door on the driver's side, replies, "I'm married, Lloyd... I got problems at home." And his partner laughs at the comment asking, "Let me guest, you both fought over the remote. right?" And Hill ignores the comment getting inside. Now, his partner gets inside, and before shutting the door, Wendy shows up. And she was wearing dark shades, a long black coat, in jeans and sneakers. And she, catching them off guard asks, "You guys have a second?" Hill then glanced at his partner says," Go talk with her, I'll wait." And his partner gets out, closing the car door asking, "Can I help you?... I know you remember my partner and I... We arrested your boyfriend, right?" Wendy was looking around, making sure no one recognized her, asks, "Can we talk somewhere inside?" And Lloyd, had nodded yes. And they went inside a lamp store, and stood at the entrance. And the customers and salespeople had seen, and began to gossip about them.

And he asked, "What's up?" And she, looking around answers, "I was hoping to run into you guys again... I come to you now, because I am tired of the abuse." Lloyd in a confused state reply, "He's in jail?... What's the problem, now?" Wendy then glanced to the left, and saw a sales lady come close, pretending to be busy. And she, with an attitude, had made eye contact asking, "What are you looking at?" And the sales lady had rolled her eyes, and walked away. Now, Lloyd calming her down, by raising his hand says, "Never mind her!... What are you asking me?" She says, "We bailed him out. Vin and I live together and have a son... I guess, what I am saying is... If he puts his hands on me again, can I call you guys?... I know you're not scared of him or Powers?" Lloyd then understood answers, "I'm a cop, if you cooperate with us... You and your son will be safe... And cops don't fear Powers by the way. "

Wendy now, feeling relieved says, "Thank you, Thank you." She then looks at his badge and gets his name. Lloyd, in thought of powers selling narcotics, asks, "I have a question for you?... Does Powers sell narcotics?" Now, Wendy begins to panic, and quickly lied answering," Of course not!" And they immediately recognized it was too quiet, and stopped talking. And they noticed all eyes, and ears were tuned into their conversation.

Lloyd then became annoyed and with a stern look says, "Can I help you, you or you with something!" And three customers, and the salespeople had gotten upset. And they then begin to gossip amongst themselves. And he looks back at Wendy asking, "What's your name by the way?" And she, not feeling comfortable about giving her name asks, "Listen, you're not going to be following me around or anything, right?" He then laughed at the remark, knowing she was nervous coming out of the store. And she, not liking his laughter, had followed, closing the entry door. And he answers, "No... If I were you, I'd leave him and Powers." And she had gotten emotional, and upset about the remark shouts, "POWERS IS MY FAMILY!... MAYBE IT WAS A MISTAKE ME TALKING TO YOU!... YOU DONT KNOW ANYTHING ABOUT US!" Lloyd then walked away to the cop car asking, "Who are you gonna call Ms.?... Who?" Hill saw and shouted, "LLOYD, YOU HAVE A MISS CALL FROM VICKY!... WHO'S VICKY?" Wendy then walked away upset, and still nervous. And Lloyd had crossed the street, and got in the car. And using sarcasm he said, "Women!" And his partner laughs at the comment, and drives off to the Police department.

Now, Feng in that same hour, was in his room looking up colleges. And he was looking at Florida, Connecticut and New York on his laptop. And he also set an appointment, regarding the dent on the car. And he then heard the doorbell ring. And gets up, and goes downstairs to see who it was. And he had gazed at the door window, and saw it was Nia. And he smirked, and rubbed his hands together, knowing he had the whole place to himself. And he opened the door saying, "What's good!... Come on in." And they kissed, as she joined hands with him. And she, being in thought of his folk had asks, "Are your folks here?... I didn't see the SUV out there." And he, closing the door answers, "Nope... I got the whole place to myself... What do you want to do?"

They then came into the living room. And she seen a family portrait of him, with his parents very young around the TV. And she stood by the TV, and held a portrait of him in Lo's arms with a toy. And she says, "I have never seen this picture before... Did your mother just put this here?" And Feng had smiled, and answered, "Here and there." Now, the doorbell had rang, and it left an awkward vibe. And she, wondering who it could be, asked," Are you expecting anyone?" He then walked away answered, "No." And he stood to the door, and saw Shepard with Bishiri. And he has an idea, opening the door asked, "You guys are looking for my dad, right?" Shepard answers," Yes... Paster told us that he was leaving early, is he here?... Or, did he take off already?... We were supposed to leave together was all." Feng answered," You guys just miss him... My mother had told him to call you guys." And they left immediately, wanting to catch Lo.

And he closed the door, and met with Nia again. She at the time was looking at the pictures hanging on the wall. And he saw and says, "To the left is my uncle Key with Lo. Below that picture, is my mother and I on Mother's Day at school... I believe I was 8 then." Feng, now becoming curious about her folks asked, "So, when am I going to meet your father?"

She then began to frown, and answers, "I rather you not meet them... When your parents had asked me all those questions, I wasn't ready Feng." And he wanting a better understanding says, "Well how can they, or I get to know you then?" Nia, given in some thought answered, "Give me time." And he saw the comment had worried her, says, "We're not out to hurt you, Nia.... Question, your here early... I mean, it's all good... I know I can never get you to come this early." And she began to smirk, answering, "I had off today, and wanted to come see you." And they smile at each other, kissing again. And she, not knowing about his plan's asks, So, what were your plans for today?" He then grabs the remote, and turns the TV on to the news answering," I was checking out colleges."

And the news anchor, had begun to talk about Steve Liang still wanted for murder. And she avoiding the news, now in a cute manner asked, "Do you still need help looking up colleges? You know ......your mother told me, that you know how to write in mandarin... Show me how you write I love you... Please !" Feng then left the remote on the table says, "Yeah, I do indeed... My mother told you I see." And she nodded yes. And she reached for the remote, and turned the TV off, and puts it back. And she reaches and joined hands with him, walking upstairs. And this destration, was all because she didn't want to see her cousin's face on the news. And she knew Feng wasn't aware and wanted to keep it that way.

They then showed up on the second floor, and she walked behind him. And as they passed the prayer room, she heard angels singing. And she had become scared of the unknown. She then hugged Feng from behind asking, "What was that?" And he, now confused had stopped near the door asked," What was what?" She releasing him, had faced him says," I heard people singing, like nothing I've ever heard before in that room... What goes on in the room?... Do you have ghost living here, Feng?" He laughed, knowing she had never heard angels sing before. And he, now calming down from laughter says," What you heard were angels singing in the prayer room... My parents had spent a lot of time in there... fear not, Nia." She then began to laugh at the remake, having a question about an angel asked, "Have you ever heard about the angel named Gabriel? He nodded yes and answers," Yes... The lord is my strength, is what his name means. EL is Lord, and Gabri is my strength... Can I tell you another thing?... When you've seen Cherubims and Seraphim's with eight wings. ...... When they fly, they leave a rainbow behind them... And, that's more than amazing. It's a beautiful thing... The last time my family and I had prayed together, we were taken up into outter space.... And we all saw spirits breeding by the moon. .. Of course, my mother would cover my eyes. .... Crazy, right?"

Nia in thought of the remark, was left speechless. They then entered the room leaving her amazed. And she then understood, that they weren't your ordinary kind of family. But, a family that knew the lord.

Now, it became Christmas day in the afternoon, with very little snow on the ground. And their neighborhood, including the Feng's residents, had shown their Christmas decorations and lights. Feng, Nia, Angel and his girlfriend named, Cassie were celebrating at the Feng residents. And they were in the living room chatting, and opening gifts from one another. And Feng glanced at Angel asking, "What did you get Cassie?" Now, Cassie was taking her time, unwrapping a gift from him. And she says, "I think it's a sweater... The box is big enough." And her personality, was down to earth, but came across as too fast at times. Angel gave no answer, but watched her with a smile. And Feng's phone had begun to vibrate at the living room table. And he reached and saw it was his mother answered, "Merry Christmas, Mom!" Now, Polly and Lo, were in the hotel room in bed relaxing. And she says, "Merry Christmas, son.... Is the Christmas decoration up?... Is Nia there?" He answers, "Yeah. Yes, it is up... Angel and his girlfriend are here too." Feng then hands the phone over to Nia. And she answers, "Hi, Mom... Yes, he gave me a lot of gifts... What did I get him?" She then turned her attention to him, and smiled at the comment made.

And Angel had seen all nine of Nia's presents, unwrapped around the tree. And he having Feng's attention had asked, "Why so many present?" And Feng laugh, and ignored the remark. And he, being given no answer, then whispered in Feng's ear asking," You're making her wait for an engagement, right?" And Feng laughed, and ignored him again. And she then hung up, and knew something was said about her based on their funny behavior. And she saw and felt the attention was on her at the time. And he then receives his phone back saying, "We're good, bro." And Feng watched Cassie, still taking her time with the gift. And he laughs, and becomes sarcastic saying, "Angel, I think she needs help!" And Angel ignores the comment, looking at the pictures on the wall. And Cassie finally finished, and saw the present was indeed a sweater. And she then gazed at Nia's gifts saying, "That's a lot of gifts." And Nia had smiled, and being sarcastic answering, "I gave him two gifts, and I receive nine!... Right?" Cassie then chucked at the remark. And the girls then went into the kitchen and Cassie asks, "What's your secret?" Now, Nia with a confuse expression asked, "What secret, I don't understand what you mean?" And she, now feels lied to says, "I think you know what I mean... How do you get your way?... And are you guys engaged yet?" She then understood, and wanted to help her out, answered, "I don't get my way, Cassie... And were not engaged... We are getting to know each other a little more, you know." And she then understood, and sat down says, "I wish I could say the same, Nia... I been throwing clues left and right." And Nia smiled at the comment, preparing to make hot cocoa for everyone.

Now, Wendy around same time, was home with her son named Mitch. And they were seated in his room enjoying a Christmas movie together. And she was watching her son's behavior, and loved how he enjoyed the main character. Mitch's character, was direct and caring. And he worried for his mother from time to time, due to her abusive relationship. Now, Vin and Ed had showed up. And Vin was drunk, with Ed being sober. And they heard the knocking, and she came to the door, seeing them through the square glass. And she then opened the door and smelled him. And she had become embarrassed and disappointed. And Vin smelled like a skunk, and was being helped coming inside. And Ed, watching the door being closed, had sat him down says, "We were drinking outside my house, and lost track of time... Sorry, Wendy." Ed then left the living room, and left him on the couch near the Christmas tree. And their son had come out of the room, and saw his father drunk. And he and his mother had made eye contact in a worried state. And he, being upset, had gone back into the room slamming the door shut. And Ed again, apologized and left. And she had seen her son's actions, locking the door. And for the sake of peace, she checks on him. And she knocks at the door calling his name. And she, not being given an answer, now entered the room. And she had glanced at Mitch, seated on the bed asking, "Do you want to go to grandmas?" And he already frustrated answers, "No... Mom, don't cover for him... He always does this!" And she then thought on the comment, looking at the window near the door. And she begun to worry about their relationship, asks," I know... Did you like your presents?" Mitch then gave her an awkward look, answers, "Yeah.... Mom, I am not a little kid anymore... I just wish he would change." And she agreed, and heard Vin calling for her. And she said, "I'll be back." And she came into the living room, and saw him in the kitchen staggering around the table. And he slurring with his words asked, "Wendy, where did you put my liquor at?" Now, Wendy concerned, had met with him says, "Sit down, you've had enough!" And he stares at her, and tries to sober up. And he says, "What do you mean I had enough, it's Christmas... Where's Mitch? ..... I left the liquor on the table, so I know somebody moved it." And she tries to get him to sit down, but he resists. And he then begins to get loud, and violent with her. And he arguably shouted, "NO !... NO!" Now, Mitch at the time, was hearing the argument and had enough. And he then came to see what was going on. And he had seen his mother, trying to stop Vin from searching in the refrigerator for liquor.

And he slammed the refrigerator door out of anger, seeing no liquor says, "I had it here yesterday, Wendy! What did you do with it?" Wendy, becoming confused yelled, "I DON'T KNOW!" Vin then pushed her up against the wall shouts, "YOURE LYING TO

ME, WHY!" Wendy then tried to calm him down by reasoning, and slowly moved away. And she, moving two feet away from him, had seen him calming down. And he was giving it some thought. She then slowly tried to hug him for comfort, and saw their son coming.

Now, Mitch have had enough, and walked into the kitchen with courage said, "I throw it out!" And Vin with a serious look had stared at him. And he then flipped the table over very anger. And he comes near loudly asking, "WHY?" And he met with Mitch ready to fight. And Wendy saw, and tried to stop him from wanting to fight their son. And she had gotten in between them, facing Vin shouting, "DON'T YOU TOUCH HIM!... DON'T TOUCH MY SON!" Vin then pushed her aside. And he reaches for his son's shirt, and draws him close, cursing him out. And she ran into their room, and went into the dresser to find a gun. And she had found the gun, and ran back aiming it at Vin. And he saw and was stunned releasing their son. And he asks, "Are you nuts?... We are Powers, we stick together to the end. Remember?" Wendy had kept the gun aim at him, in a no-nonsense manner. He then realized she was very serious, says, "I was just playing with him... I didn't mean it." She then slowly lowers the gun, believing him. And he had walked over to her saying, "You don't want to do this, Wendy." And he seen her calm down, and within seconds he slapped her to the ground. And the gun and Wendy were a cross from each other. And their son, in shock, had seen his mother on the ground bleeding from the mouth. And he with rage, immediately attacks his father from behind. And Vin saw him coming, and forcefully pushed him up against the sink counter. And Mitch was knocked down, and had seen his mother get back up again. And she had pointed the gun at Vin again, with tears. Now, Mitch on the ground, had seen and shouted, "MOM!... IT'S NOT WORTH IT! PLEASE!" And Vin staring at her says, "Let's all relax." And she shouts, "NO!... YOURE NOT GONNA PUT YOUR HANDS ON ANYONE ELSE AGAIN!" Mitch watching his mother pull the trigger shouts, "MOM!! .... NO !! "

And she shot Vin twice in the heart, watching him fall dead close to the table bleeding. And she immediately dropped the gun, and sat down on the floor crying. And her son had walked over, and sat next to his mother, and they hugged out of comfort.

And the neighbors outside the apartment all heard the gun go off. And the neighbors inside had come out, wanting to know what had happen. And one lady had called 911 to makes sure the police investigate the shooting.

5 minutes later, they heard a knock at the door. And they heard a man's voice asking, "Is everything alright in there?... We heard gun shots?" And Mitch says, "Mom, we have to give an answer." She nodded and continued crying. And he got up from the floor, to answer the door. And he saw it was their neighbor from next door, and greeted him. And the neighbor in concern, asked, "Young man, what happen?... My wife and I heard gunshots !... Where's your folk, and who's that crying?" Before Mitch could answer, everyone heard police sirens coming close by. Mitch then closed the door, so no one could see what had happened. And the neighbor felt his behavior was awkward, and began to walk away.

Now, Wendy was on the news within an hour, and everyone was watching it. And the news reporter says," Vin London, lord of the biker gang called Powers... Was killed this afternoon due to self-dense by his girlfriend, Wendy Green... And Mitch, their twelve-year-old son, says they were attacked. And he also said to the police, that it was in self-defense... And Vin was released not too long ago... And the reason being, he had threatened two police officers at a sports bar... And this is the news we have regarding Powers. "The camera then showed the news anchor seated. And the news anchor says," Well... I sure hope everyone is safe at home, and enjoying their Christmas. The Mayor of New Haven gave a speech early this afternoon at city hall. In regards to criminal activity. And the mayor wants to start the new year by increasing the arrest, wishing us all a safe and merry Christmas... We will be right back with more news. "

Steve at the time, was in the warehouse watching the news around the pool table. And Mia had met with him holding a bottle of champagne, with two champagne glasses. And she smiled at him, sitting everything down at the pool table. Steve watching her open the bottle, was disturbed by the mayor's comment. And she handed him a glass, and they gave a toast smiling at each other. And he then felt, he needed to make an example out of the mayor very soon as a reminder, of who he is.

Now, Feng saw the news in the living room. And everyone else was around the Christmas tree chatting. And he had recognized Wendy, and looks over at Angel asking," Angel?... You remember the big dude, throwing his lady to the ground at that sports bar?" And he had met with Feng, and thought about the remark. He then remembered said, "How could I forget!" Feng says, "She killed her man on Christmas day!... That's crazy, bro!" Angel replies, "I'm sorry to hear that... Nobody should put their hands on anyone." Nia with Cassie then came over to find out what had happened.

And the news immediately came back on. And Nia heard the fellas talk about it again, and immediately started to have flash backs of her father yelling at her. Now, Cassie takes notice that something wasn't right, watching her zone out. And she calls for her attention asking, "Nia, you, ok?" She then snaps out of it, and quickly answers, "Yeah, I am... You want to hear some sounds... Feng, you have music in your room, right?" He, being put out on the spot answers, "Yeah!... What do you want to hear?" And she then looked at Cassie, dancing around says, "Something to dance to!" And Cassie at the time, was trying to understand her mood. And Angel, now wanting Cassie's attention, called her into the kitchen. And she met with him asking, "Where's the alcohol at?" And he had laughed, knowing she didn't know better said, "This is a house of God's love." And she looked at him confused, and didn't get it. And he said, "Feng's dad is Pastor Lo Feng." And she held her hand over her mouth embarrassed, not knowing. And she replies," I had no idea... Where are his folks from?" Angel then sat with her at the table answered, "Who cares."

Now, Nia at the time, had sat on Feng's lap on the couch, looking at the window. And she saw light snow showers, and was in thought of Feng. And they looked at each other, and kissed and giggle. And she says, "Merry Christmas, babe." And Angel from the kitchen loudly asked, "WHERE'S THE MUSIC, BRO?" And they begin to laugh at the remark, forgetting about the music. And they all stayed up very late drinking hot cocoa, and unwrapping more gifts.

The next morning, around 8:20 am at the Police Department. Detective Mary was coming from Lewis's office, and met Lugo in the hallway. And he asks, "What's new?... How was your Christmas?" And she smiled and answers," My Christmas was great... Roy, is willing to cooperate with us to get a lesser sentence... In discussion, we told him that we have the footage... So, he felt he should come clean... The problem we are having now, is finding out where everyone lives... All the addresses of the crew provided by Roy are now vacant." Lugo becoming sarcastic says," It's because you came to Roy's apartment... They're still in town." Now, Lugo, with a question regarding detective Miller asked," Question.... You and Miller in the car... He was willing to kill you, right?" Mary thought the question was rather odd. And she, given it some thought, had remembered his face in shock of being shot at. And the police then raided the car armed, seeing her come out of the passenger seat. And she had removed her wig, and told what had happened. And the police indeed, had found drugs in the back seat of the car. Mary then snaps out of it and answers," Yes… He drew first, and slow detective." Mary then walked away. And he saw and gathered his thoughts.

Now, Renee early that afternoon was at the salon, and had gotten her hair done. And she walked over to the register to talk with the owner named Barbara, about setting another appointment. And she paid by card, and received it back, placing it in her purse. And Barbara says, "You know… I never saw your hair blonde before, Renee… I know I am not your stylist… Toni is." And she smiled at the comment, and was in thought of her next schedule. Barbara then asked," How was your Christmas by the way?" And she in thought, answers," It was good, lots of seafood… Better when mom was around. My father, sister and I… Come to think of it, had a very good Christmas… How was yours?" Barbara answered,"My husband and I had family come over, and saw the grands." Renee in thought of her grandkids said," Awww!" And she continued talking.

Toni then heard a noise, and curiously left her station to the front door. And she seen a black sports car being towed, and thought it was odd. And she asked, "Anyone own a black sports car?" Renee believing it was her car, quickly says, "Barbara!… I'll be right back!" And the ladies had watched her run out, and gossip about the situation. Now, Renee from behind, met with the cops, watched the car get towed. And she upset shouts, "HEY!… WHAT ARE YOU TWO DOING!" And they then turned around and saw her. And Lloyd, being amazed to see her again, counted it a prayer answered. And Hill asks, "Can I help you?" Renee frowning at them asked, "Why did you two tow my car?… My insurance is paid. Where is he going with my car?" Lloyd saw that she was steamed answers, "We received a complaint about a black sports car in this plaza... Guy says, it's been parked here for three days." And she asks, "By what guy?... Who?... I only had been here for an hour. So, it can't be me... Right?" Renee and Hill begin to argue. And Lloyd looked to the right, and saw another black sports car that looked the same.

Renee again asked, "Where did he take my car?" Now, Lloyd looking back are her asked," What's your name?" She then gazed at him, with a confuse expression answered, "Renee, why?" Lloyd then pointed to the right asking, "Is that your car?" She then looked and got embarrassed, forgetting where she had parked. And she says, "I am so sorry you guys, Sorry." And she walked away very fast, still embarrassed. And Lloyd seen an opportunity, and told his partner to give him a minute. And he ran, and caught up to her asking, "Have we met before." And she stopped and answered," I don't know you." And he, charming her up with a smile had asked," Listen, would I be wrong for asking you for your number... I'm Lloyd, by the way." She thought about it, seeing how handsome he was answered," Why not." And they exchange numbers by phone. And she, checking him out says, "I had never given my number nor dated a cop before." And his partner at the time couldn't believe Lloyd. And he had thought to himself, that Lloyd would break her heart. Lloyd then glanced at his partner asked, "So, you're not seeing anyone, right?" And she answers, "No. I don't play games... And I don't suppose, you'll tell me who file a complaint, right?"

Lloyd attention was now caught by his partner waving. And he answers, "Complaint?... The manager at the restaurant to your right was complaining. I got to go, but... I will call you later, ok?" Renee nodded with a smile. Barbara then came out and met with her out of concern. And she then gave her a reassurance, that she was alright.

And Lloyd had walked away, and came to the patrol car door says, "I'm dreaming, bro." Hill replied, "Dream when you get home, not now." And his partner noticing his behavior, quickly said, "Jealous." And they now got inside the patrol car. And Hill answers, "Jealous?... Lloyd please, every time I turn around there is a woman involve with you." And Lloyd ignoring the remark said, "Shut up and drive, Hill." And hill starts the car up saying, "And, you never answered my question on who Vicky was." Lloyd becoming annoyed answered," Vicky is my ex." And Hill knew his partner was annoyed says, "This new one you're talking to now... I overheard her say that she doesn't play games... You saw the car she drives; she could've said no." And Lloyd thought about the comment looking at the window. And they left the plaza, and approached a red light, headed to the police department.

Chapter 8

Now, earlier that afternoon, Lugo was all in his feelings about the case. And he, without a wire, and Terry had arrived at the wine store to get orders. And the manager, back from vacation, was in the backroom receiving new wine at the time. And the cashier, scheduled to work was a crew member. And he stood near the backroom door, watching for the customers, and the manager. Now, the detective walking to the entrance had stopped, and saw the fellas listening to Richie. And Richie in disguise, had seen him says," Hey... Steve wants to talk to you... I had just got off the phone a minute ago with him... I'm taking you there now."

And he then dismissed the fellas, leaving with Lugo passing customers. And the customers came, and stood near the entry door looking at the wine. And the crew following orders was leaving. And the cashier had played his part, coming over to help customers in need. Now, Richie had gone in the car, reaching for a mask in the glove compartment. And he opened, and closed it back with a mask saying, "Put this on... And keep your head down in the backseat." Lugo then opened and closed the back door. And he leaned down receiving the mask, and puts it on. Now, Richie begins to drive around. And he drove for a half an hour, fooling Lugo regarding the distances. And they arrived at a vacant warehouse, behind another vacant building. And he had drove in the back alley in reverse, and parked. Now, the guard named Steven saw, and was at the door. And he told the boss by phone, that he has guests. And Richie at the time reached for the mask, and removed it from his face. And he then told Lugo to get out, and together they came out the car. And they approached the door, ready for the meeting. And the guard only frisked Lugo, and found nothing. And the detective thought him being frisk was rather odd, but went along with it. And the guard opened and closed the door, knowing they're clean. And because of that, only then, could they enter in.

And they came inside, making their way to the hallway into the main room, seeing Steve at a pool table. Now, the warehouse was one floor with three cameras above. And there was one office, one TV, a restroom, one armed guard, one sentry safe and a refrigerator.

Now, Mia the watcher, had seem them and immediately went into Steve office leaving the door open. And their boss saw them says, "Lugo, grab a pool stick and hear me." And he walked over, and reached for the only pool stick, up against the pool table. And Richie saw a bottle of alcohol, and cups above the refrigerator. And he removed the disguise and walked over to drink. Now, Steve had started a new game, and made the first shot. And he, watching the balls all scattered asked, "Do you carry a gun when you watch for the cops?" Steve then glanced at him, knowing it was his turn to shoot. And Lugo answers, "I do… You remember how we met, right?… Boss?" He then made a strike, and nearly got the black ball in. And he felt relieved, and waited for his turn again. Now, Steve had seen him look around, and with sarcasm asked, "You see anything you like, Lugo?… The safe over to the left, was the money my brother provided us… Before he, and a few others had gotten killed. Not including what we collect... I'm telling you this for a reason... I almost wanna ask where did you get your gun from." And the detective ignores the comment, watching him focus on the blue ball to the left. Steve then asked, "Ever kill anyone, Lugo?"

Richie then stared at him, putting the cup down on the refrigerator says, "Hey... That's a good question." Now, Lugo watched him hit the blue ball around, and a couple fell in the hole answers, "No... But I have shot someone before, why?" Steve then waved Richie over, and waited for his turn again. And he glanced at Lugo focus asking, "If I ask you to kill this man, would you?" Now, Lugo feeling confuse quickly asked, "You're asking me to kill, Richie?" Richie then met with them, and begins to frown at the remark. And he not understanding says, "Boss, what's this all about?" And he looked at the balls said, "It's your turn, Lugo." And the detective tried to understand making the shot, and one ball went in. And he stood straight up, and curiously asks, "What are you asking me?" Now, Steve with a smirk answers, "Alright... Richie lied to me about the cop situation. And the footage of the murder at the shop was televised." Now, Richie was shocked and immediately kneeled. And he begged for mercy, holding Steve's right leg shouts, "I WAS NOT THERE WHEN THEY TOOK THE FOOTAGE!... POWERS ATTACK ME, REMEMBER!" Lugo looking at Richie loudly asked, "HOW DID THE POLICE KNOW WHERE TO LOOK?"

And Richie, worried for his life, gave no answer. And Steve says, "You were way too nerves about the cops... You should had erased or gotten rid of the footage like I said, Richie!... You deserve to die!" And Richie starts to cry saying, "I wasn't thinking!... Please, don't kill me!" Now, Lugo loudly asked, "WHY DIDNT YOU TELL HIM, RICHIE?" And he again, gave no answer, crying. And Steve then took a breather, asking, "How do we make this right, right?"

Lugo waiting on Steve, asks, "You want me to kill him then?" Now, Richie not knowing what to think, loudly says, "BOSS, LET ME PROVE MY LOYALTY TO YOU AGAIN!" And the detective watched, and wondered what Steve really wanted. And he saw that Steve was disgusted, and wanted no parts of him. And Steve disappointed said, "I know you're a wanted man just like me... Don't ever lie to me again!... Now, leave you two... Before I change my mind." Now, Richie had gotten up, thanking him a few times. And the guard then came close.

Now, Steve watching them leave, shouted, "LUGO!" And they stopped, and gave their full attention. And he said, "Get ready to kill, and don't you fail me... Leave!" And the detective nodded in agreement, and they left. Now, Mia comes out of the office overhearing everything, and looks at Richie. And she made eye contact with Steve. And he, turning his back, had given a devilish smirk, regarding Richie's fate. And she nodded at ease, understanding the smirk, and gone back into the office. And the guard had walked with them down the hall, opening the door. And Steven was closing the door shut, as they had passed him on the phone. Now, Richie then put the disguise back on, walking to the car deep in thought. And the detective from a distance, had looked straight down. And he saw a cheap store named Cheaper's Keepers. And the store was across the street. And he had kept that in mind, knowing they were behind a warehouse, unsure of the city. And when they had gotten inside the car, he was handed the mask again. And Richie now embarrassed and insecure says, "I should had told him. And had erase the evidence... But why did he let me live?" And the detective with the mask on, begins to lay down in the backseat answers, "I don't know why... He needs you, I guess." Now, Lugo thought about him being asked would he kill Richie... And he then, didn't know how to take to him, moving forward. Now, Richie had drove back to the wine store, overthinking the whole situation. And he had thoughts of Lugo being asked to kill him. And he knew now, to keep an eye on him.

And when they arrived back at the wine store, Lugo had gone inside to the restroom. And Richie was in the parking lot, smoking a cigarette. Now, Lugo saw no one and locked the door, calling Lewis. And the sergeant answered, asking," Lugo?... What's up?" And he answers," Listen, I saw Steve... The guards, a woman, a safe inside a warehouse." Now, Lewis wanting to know more asked," Okay... Terry was with you, right?" And the detective, feeling uneasy answered," I wasn't wired, and no." Now, Lewis in a loud manner shouted," WHY?... YOUR A DETECTIVE, IT'S WHAT YOU DO!... YOU'RE BEGGING ME TO FIRE YOU, LUGO !!... And the detective interrupts, saying," I was frisk at the door... The warehouse is behind an old building, and across from it was a cheap store. Richie gave me a mask to put on... We'll talk later." Lugo then heard a loud knock at the door. And he tells his boss he had to go, and hung up. And he unlocked the door, and saw a customer and Chi come in. Now, Chi seeing him thought it was odd, asked, "Why was the door locked? And he answered," I'm in between girls, and didn't want you to hear it. And Chi laughed, and told him to go watch for the cops. And he nodded and went outside, ready to report anything.

Now, Steve later in the afternoon wore a disguise, and drove around. And he showed up to the other side of town, wearing shades. And he surprisingly saw Alex coming out of a corner store, and stopped. And he called out his name, and got his attention. And Alex had walked across the street unsure of who he was. He then recognized and met with him asking, "Steve?... What are you doing here?" And he smiled and said, "Get in." And the person behind had blew the horn a couple times, watching everything. Steve then takes off and approaches a red light. And Alex already nervous, had asked, "What's up?" And his cousin smirked at the remark asking, "How's the family?" And Alex, scratching his head answers, "Nia and I are fine... Where are you taking me?" Now, the light had turned green. And he made a left turn into a plaza, full of many restaurants, and parked. And he answers, "Listen, I know you know that I am wanted... And I know that you're nervous... But, we are still blood." And Alex, not understanding him asked," What do you want?" Now, Steve upset with the comment, arguably answers, "I know you think I'm the bad apple of the family, but I'm not... I want to do something for you." And Alex, out of nervousness, says, "I can't get into any trouble... I got a house and a life." And Steve out of remembrance, asks, "You like your job?" And Alex gave no answer, looking straight headed. And he reached and opened the glove compartment, and handed Alex fifty grand. And he seen his facial expression in shock over the money. And he closing the compartment says, "Family takes care of family. I'll bring you back... Buy Nia something." And Alex, still in shock replies, "Steve, I don't know what else to say... Thanks, man!" And he said," How about you come and work for me." And Alex looks at the money, thinking on the comment. And Steve knew then, he had him leaving the plaza. And Alex with a made-up mind said," Alright... I'm in... I'm in Steve." Now, Steve with a smirk, goes back to the corner store, and tells Alex to follow him. And Alex got in his car and followed.

Twenty minutes later, they arrived at a closed club. And Steve had parked in the lot, surrounded by the crew. And the detective had seen Alex, not knowing who he was. And Steve then whispered in Lucky's ear, giving him orders. And afterwards, he got into another car with Alex and left. Now, Lugo looking at Lucky ask," Who's the guy with Steve?" And Lucky answered," That's his cousin, Alex... And he's about to join the crew." And he nodded at the comment made, keeping his name in mind. And Alex that day, indeed became an official crew member.

Now, Renee around that time, had just arrived home from food shopping. And she closing the car door, came to the entry door with the keys, holding a bag of produce. And she had seen the garage door closed assuming her sister was home, yells, "CHI CHI, YOU HOME?" And she didn't hear anything, so she opened and closed the door. And her phone begins to ring in her back pocket. And she checked and saw it was Lloyd's number, holding the bag with one arm. And she smiled, placing her phone to her shoulder answering, "Lloyd?" Now, Lloyd voice, in good spirit reply, "I told you I would call you… Listen, what are you doing New Year Eve?" Now, Renee had gone into the kitchen sitting the keys, and bag down on the table. And she goes into the living room removing her sneakers, and sat on the couch. And with her phone to the ear, she answered, "I most likely, will be with my family on New Year Eve." Lloyd says, "Family comes first you know… So, when can I see you?" Renee had smiled at the remark, answers, "Any time after New Year's, I guess." And he paused for a minute, and says," I want to get to know you… And have an awesome time with ya." Now, Lloyd heard her laugh at the comment, so he continues to charm her up. And they officially agreed to a date, after conversating for twenty-five minutes.

December 31 of 2017 at 11:45 pm at Feng's house. Feng, Nia, Angel and Cassie were in the living room watching TV, and waiting for the ball to drop. And they were in conversation with each other, with a plate of holiday cookies at the table. And Angel, with his girlfriend's camera, had taken pictures of them all. And he says, "I have a feeling, that 2018 is gonna be awesome, bro!… I'll send you the pictures later." And he sat down the camera near the cookies. Now, Cassie becoming curious about them asks, "Awesome because were together or…?" And she waited for his answer, watching him eat a cookie. And he laughed at the comment saying, "Cassie, I want you… But I am not ready for marriage right now." And she begins to roll her eyes with an attitude at the remark. And she sat with Nia and Feng on the couch. Now, Nia had glanced at her being upset asks, "Cassie, you, ok?" And she answered, "I will be." And Feng reached, and held the remote from the table said, "Let's see what else is on." And Nia quickly replies, "Don't turn or you'll miss the ball. "And he puts the remote back, and was now in thought of her brother. So, he asked, "Nia, where is your brother?" And she shrugs at the comment, and answered, "Who knows."

Now It became 11:59 pm. And Angel with Feng had stood around the TV. And everyone but Cassie, had begun to count down into the New Year.

And afterward, they had celebrated watching the ball drop. And Cassie was still upset with Angel, and looked away. And he tries to cheer her up saying, "Happy New Year, babe!" And she got up, and went into the kitchen to avoid him. And he, not knowing what to say to her, had gone to Feng. And he said, "I'm not ready for marriage, bro." And Feng answers, "If she is rushing you… let her go, bro… You can't rush marriage." Now, Nia then got up from the couch and kissed him. And she giggling, says, "Happy New Year, babe! "And Feng smiling, answered, "Back at cha!" And Angel watched, and in a sarcastic manner said, "See, that's what I want man."

Now, Cassie near the door had shouted, "I AM READY TO GO HOME, ANGEL!" And Angel then reached for the camera, and goes to the kitchen saying, "See you guys later." And Feng laugh at the situation saying, "It's a new year, bro. If you're not ready…" Angel had nodded, and understood, and left with Cassie. And they sat back, and relaxed on the couch. Now, Nia had rested her head on his shoulder, watching TV asking, "What does 2018 have in store for us?" And Feng gazed at her answering, "We have each other... And that's all that matters, love." And they kissed and continued watching TV, holding hands.

Now, before it became January 3 of 2018. These affairs had happened. Wendy had cooperated with Mary, giving information for her family's protection. And she and her son at the time, were living with her older sister named Judy Green. And Powers would have their meeting, but were in need of a leader. And Ed was now voted in the new Lord of Powers to keep order. And he, being motivated by fast money, had made a lot of errors. And he at the time, did business with Mr. Smith. And this now led to the fall of Powers. And Ed and the rest of the members had got busted for selling narcotics to detective Ronald. Now, Ronald had played the role of a drug dealer, with a crew of cops leading to a successful raid.

Now, the transaction had happened one evening, behind Ed's gun range building. And Mr. Smith, and all his crew were present during the transaction. And when the raid had happened, Cowell his righthand man, thought he could get the boss away in time, but had failed at the attempt. And the cops were all around them, armed and ready. And Ed was later questioned by Peter at the police station, and received no answer. And Mr. Smith was questioned next, but wouldn't talk without a lawyer. And the gun range company he owned, was under investigation, and later shut down.

Now, concerning the Feng's in Maimi Florida. The Feng's, the church members, the musicians and the deacons were invited to a lot of revival services. And the bishop of the church had loved the way he taught the word of God. And he also loved the way Polly had dance with a flag, and the deacons sung. And every time she danced, Lo thought of Feng. And he loved seeing his beautiful wife in her worship outfit throwing the flag up, and catching it. And the Bishops and Pastors that came to the revivals had invited them to they're churches. Now, Lo was feeling overwhelmed at the time, and was ready to come back home. And it was also around this time, that the feng's began to have security with them .

Now, Maggie had begun to hear a lot of complaints from Eric about the crew activities, in and out of the store. And her character made her a very determined businesswoman, that wanted no drama. And she began visiting the store to stop the heat.

And she one day caught the cashier crew member, selling drugs to an underage girl. And she immediately fired him, and got threatened. And she told them to never to come back to her store again. And the cashier later regretted it, remembering she was related to Steve. And he then went to his apartment in fear of her telling Steve. And he went into the bedroom, and opened the dresser for a gun. And with tears, he thought about his life putting the gun to his head. And he pulled the trigger, and had committed suicide. And the situation was on the news, and everyone saw. And Mary and Peter were then on the job. And when the detectives came to the apartment, they had questioned the landlord. And the landlord told everything, and gave them the employer. And Maggie was indeed questioned by the detectives; and they already knew he was with Steve.

Now, Steve, in his office had a serious conversation with the investor over the phone. And he spoke about the strippers that work for him, waiting for his orders. And they knew where to look regarding beautiful young American women. And he fully convinced the investor to work with him, despite being wanted. And he also received calls from his top guys, about being watched by cops at the gas stations. And they were told to lie low, and wait for further instructions. Now, Mary and Peter then were told to go investigate the two gas stations. And they came with questions, and got nothing from the owners. And the detectives knew by their body language, that the owners were in fear for their lives.

And they denied anything to do with Steve's crew. And it was during this time, when Lucky one afternoon, behind the store, told and shown his gun to Lugo , saying, This was the gun used to kill that Garcia chick on the news. And the detective watching him take aim with the gun answered,Really?

Now, one afternoon on the third of January. Lugo was off duty leaving a supermarket. And he with a bag of groceries, had recognized Alex with a woman. And he, being unfamiliar with Nia, kept watching. And the Yung's at the time, had a cart full of groceries close to the car. Lugo then hid around cars, placing the bag down using his phone for photos. And after they had loaded the car, he saw them leave. And he, with the bag, rushed to the car and began to speed. And he had caught up, following them slowly to their house. And he took pictures of everything passing the house, and parked two houses down. And he, through the side mirror, had seen them go inside with the groceries. And Lugo, within seconds ready to leave, had seen her again closing the front door. And she began to walk away, and stood near facing the street. And he, becoming confused, began to relax himself. And he continued to watch when he could. Now, she saw a car, she had been waiting for come. And he immediately turned around, and took a picture of the man being Feng. And he, watching them leave, took a breather and left. And he later came to the police department to show and tell Lewis.

Now, two days later in the afternoon, Feng was waiting for Nia to come out of the clothing store. And he stood around the car, having a flashback of the spring in 2015. And it began with him being in the house, with his father seated on the living room coach. Now, Lo at the time, was waiting for a very important phone call, asks, "How's everything?" And Feng answered, "Things are good. I've been thinking about college?... I want to go to college." And Lo asks "What field?" He answered, "IT, dealing with computers." Now, Lo saw his son's desire, in his expression says, "Do it... Live life with no regrets... I've always been proud of you, and will always be... And let nothing stop you, son!" And Feng chucked, said, "I hear you." Feng then came out of the flashback, still waiting.

Now, Angel, driving inside the plaza, had seen him. And he from a distance shouted, "HEY, FENG!" And Feng then saw him shouts, "WHAT'S UP, ANGEL?... HOW'S EVERYTHING, MAN?" Now, Angel then stopped and watched for cars passing by. And he, having the right of way goes, and parked behind Feng. And Angel closing the door, had met with him answers," Good, good... Guess I wasn't the only one, with shopping on my mind." And he greeted Feng with a handshake, saying, "I've been seeing this girl named Amanda... Weve been talking for a few days now. And she's a good girl, not like the other one... Rushing marriage." Feng had chucked, and watched customers come in and out the store answers, "Word... That's, what's up." And Angel saw he was focused on the clothing store. And he, not seeing Nia now asked, "Where is Nia?... Is she still a secretary?" And Feng smiled, and points to the clothing store answers, "Shopping... And yes, she is." And Angel nodded, with another question in mind. Now, Nia then came out of the store, smiling with three bags of clothes. And she, smiling at Angel said," Hi, Angel!" Now, Angel then came and met with her, grabbing two bags. And Feng then opened the back door, and was making room. And Angel begins to place the bags in the backseat asking, "Are you a bouncer anywhere else?" And Feng thought the question was odd, reaching for the keys in his pocket answering, "Nope... Thanks for your help, brah... I'll check with you later." Angel had remembered their photos were in his car said," Give me a minute." And he went to his car going in says," I got your photos, give me a minute." And he reached into the glove compartment taking the photos, and met with them. Now, Nia, putting the last bag away, receives the photos, and loved what she saw. And Angel, not wanting to hold them up said, "Alright, man." And they left the plaza while he watched.

Now, Nia had reached to the backseat for one of the bags. And she was hoping, he'd like the sweater she bought him. And he, watching the road had wonder what she had bought ask, "What did you get?" And he get's a call before she could answer. And he grabbed his phone from the center console, and saw it was Lloyd. And Feng answering, heard him ask, "Feng, where are you?" And Feng, missing the left turn, saw another turn coming up, and made the turn. And he then answers, "I'm with my girl headed home, why?" Now, Nia had notice he missed the turn, asks, "Who's, that?"

Now, she gets a call, hearing music from the purse on her lap. And she opened the purse, seeing her brother's name. And closed the purse ignoring the call. And Alex at the time, was at the entry of a club. And he began to wonder why she didn't answer, and hung up. Now, Chi then came out of the club, and met with him asking, "Everything, alright?" And he in concern, had put the phone in his back pocket responds, "It will be." And Chi laughs, and tells him to come inside. And they went inside to party.

Now, Feng then arrived at the house, and was still on the phone. And after he had parked, she bought everything inside leaving the front door open. And Lloyd in a sarcastic manner says, "You should join the force and become a cop, bro. By the way..... Stay away from Howard Ave... Because we're watching everything!" Feng, now coming out the car says," I'm good, bro... If I see anything suspicious, I'll let you know... Peace." He then hung up, and closed the car door. And he thought on the conversation, walking inside the house closing the front door. Now, Feng, entering the living room, saw her on the couch going through the bags. And Nia saw his facial expression, showing he was worried and tired. So, she in concern had asked, "Is everything, alright?... Who was that?" He answers," My friend Lloyd, he's a cop... He's just looking out for me." And Nia thought it strange, says, "You're not a cop?" And he in remembrance, answers, "No, I'm not.... He's saying there's something going on at Howard Ave, and to stay away from it." And she in thought asked, "Howard Ave?" And she having some idea, immediately changing the subject. And she then continued to look for the sweater, in the bags asking," How's mama Polly?... I haven't seen her for some time now." And he then sat next to her and respond, "She's doing good... They're in Florida, remember?" She then laughed and nodded. And she found, and held up the sweater asking, "Do you like this sweater, or... ?" Feng, now looked at the sweater, had felt that the style was outdated. Now, the style of the sweater had shown six thunderbolts, in different colors. He then got up from the couch, and smiled. And he begins to act tried saying, "I'm going to bed now." And he immediately walked away. And Nia saw, and became irritated that he gave no answer saying, "Feng!... Feng!... Come here, mister!" And she followed him upstairs to the room, and talked about the sweater until he'd agree to wear it. And he, indeed, didn't like the sweater.

Now, Lloyd that same evening, was on his first date with Renee at an Italian restaurant. And the waiter that had seated them said," he'll be back." And they removed their coats, and gave it to another waiter nearby. And they were dressed casually, and had admired each other's taste sitting down. And she had sat her small purse on the table, and became comfortable saying, "Finally, I get a chance to know Chase." And he laughed and said, "You're the only woman I'd chase." And she smiled, and gave the comment some thought asked, "Is that your way of saying I'm beautiful?" Now, she took a sip of water from her glass, waiting for an answer. Lloyd answers, "Yes, it is.... What do you do by the way?" And she, placing the glass down answers, "I'm not working right now... But when I do, it will be under my father."

And he becoming curious asked "And, who's your father?" Renee answers, "Sylvester is his name... My grandfather, had owned an architecture company called De Nino's Pillar. So, artwork and building things... My family comes to mind." And he became intrigued, with what was said. And he, not wanting to worry her says," I hope you don't think I am seeing you for the money?" And she laughed and answers, "No silly... You mean my grandfather's money." And they laugh at the comment. And after calming down from laughter. She wondered, was he driven by money asked," Does money make you happy?" And he smirks at the remark answering," Well... Money doesn't make me happy. And money don't give me joy... But, it makes it so close... That I don't know the difference." Now, Renee surprised by his answer had laugh, and in a sarcastic manner says," WoW!... I've never heard that one before." Now, Lloyd, taking advantage of a good time gently reached, and joined hands with her says, "Renee, I want to be your man... I want a future with you." And she becoming curious about him asked," So, tell me about yourself?... Who you are?" He then chuckled at the remark answers," Well, I grew up with no sibling... My parents divorced when I was three... And I love hockey and fast cars... Me, I am just a guy that likes to help people out. Which is why I became a cop... But, I haven't met that special someone yet... Like you Renee, that's what you are." And they then look enthusiastically at each other. And the waiter then came over asking "Are we ready to order?" And Lloyd removing his hand, answered," Ladies first." And she told the waiter what she wanted; Lloyd ordered after. And they continued conversating, and their food came twenty minutes later.

Now, Lloyd after the date had asked, and receives their coats from the waiter. And he helped her put the coat back on again, and paid. And they came outside and stood at the entry door.

And he, after a few seconds, took a chance asking," Renee, I really like you... I was wondering, well..." Renee with her purse, was blushing at the remark. And she, out of curiosity asked," Well?" He then chuckled and asks," Would you be my girlfriend?... I don't know if I am moving too fast for you... I don't wanna lose you, Renee." And she smiled, answering," Yes... Yes, I'd like to be your girlfriend. "Now, Lloyd was amazed and took a breather. And he, with joy in his voice said," Great! Were official then!... I'll walk you to your car." And she had thought to herself, his behavior and mannerism was adorable. And they crossed the street and walked to her car. And she reached into her purse, and held the key button to unlock it. And Lloyd had held the door open for her, goin in and had closed it. And she rolls the window down with the engine on, and said," Call, me." And she left the parking lot, and made a right turn. And he saw her leave, reaching into his pocket for the car key. And he, still amazed, had left.

It then became the morning time, and Nia came home. And she had seen Alex at the garage cleaning out his car. And she parked behind him, and went out to meet with him. And she, with her arms crossed looking down says, "I saw you had called... I wasn't feeling well yesterday... That's why I didn't answer. I was at my girlfriend's house last night... How's everything?" Now, Alex was reading her body language, and knew her actions. And she was avoiding eye contact, ready to go inside. And he answers, "Things are good. Question?... Are you seeing anyone?" Now, Nia then looked at him puzzled, and felt awkward. And she immediately saw a black sports car pull up, and parked in front. Now, Steve wearing a bearded disguise with Mia had stopped by. And Alex, wondering who it was, came to the car. And Steve then rolled down the window and said," Mr. Yung!" And he then got out of the car and embraced him with a handshake. And Alex then recognized him asking, "What's up, what brings you here?" Now, Steve wore a black hoodie with dark shade, looking around the area answers, "We're family is what brings me here." And he seen Nia and waved. And he replies," Alex, walk with me." And Alex concerned had followed says, "Alright, what's up?" And after a few steps, Steve then faced him. And he, in a low tone voice says, "It's no secret that I lead the crew! We have money and don't kill... But, what I'm saying to you is... I want you more involved in the crew." Now, Alex thought the comment was odd replies, "Wait!... I'm already a crew member, what are you asking me?" And Steve says, "Family takes care of family. I don't kill people. But... What if we must kill." Now, Alex thought about the comment given no answer. And Steve, having mixed feelings about him says," I won't put you through like the ones I recruited. I remember how you two grew up... And I can give you a better life, than your father did." And he saw Alex give it some thought. And he then walked away, and drove off. And he knew that he had planted a seed in Alex. And Alex, still in thought, had seen his sister go inside the house. And his thoughts were now about his life.

Now, Maggie at that same hour, had come to check on the store again with Eric. And they at the time, were doing a walk through on the floor. And Eric worried says, "Maggie, I got to tell you... These thugs come inside the store, and never buy anything but hold quick meetings... One of my new cashiers had told me, they're always in and out the store... If they aren't buying anything, what should I do?" Maggie asked, "Are these regulars?" And he answers, "Yes, again they don't buy anything. We do get a lot of business in the neighborhood... And my cashiers say they hear the name Steve, a lot." Now, Maggie then stopped walking, and faced him. And she knew he didn't know anything about her nephew says, "I will review the cameras, don't worry... I will take it from here." Eric then felt relieved, and introduced her to the cashier that spoke up. And he then saw and called out the name Tiffany, waving her over. She then left the register and greeted Maggie. Now, Maggie then told Eric, she had a meeting to attend and left. And Eric thought nothing of it, and headed to the back room. And the cashier didn't know what to think, walking back to the register. And as Maggie approached her car, she knew that she'd had to meet with Steve at some point and time. Hoping to put an end to the disturbing.

And later that day, at the Feng's resident's garage. Feng and Angel were talking. And Angel says "Feng, you don't talk much about your father?" And Feng, putting his hands in his pocket, answered, "What you want to know, how he met the deacons ?" And Angel begins to cross his arms, said, "We can start with the deacon's... But, I wanna know a little more about Lo." Now, Feng in thought, begins to answers, "My father... He led those men, at the same time to Christ preaching from home... And they all have a story to tell... Who knew, they'd be deacons, right?... My father, before that time, had thought of becoming an aircraft pilot." Now, Angel, becoming amazed says, "I didn't know that... I respect your family, bro." And he answers, "I know you do... Your always over the house showing respect." Now, Angel in thought of his maiden name asks, "How does Polly feel about the name Winters?" And he thought on the comment and answers," My mom still honors my maiden's name. When my birth mother was young, she couldn't take care of me... Polly stepped in." And Angel responds, "You don't have to explain yourself, we go way back". Now, Angel then in remembrance, of an invite asked ,"What are you doing tonight?" And Feng in thought asked," Why, What's up?" And he, having Feng's attention, answers, "I was invited to a party tonight... You should come, bro!" Feng began to smile at the remark. And Angel waiting for an answer says," I see you smiling." And he answers, "Only if the Mrs. is down." Angel being in a funny manner, responds, "Well, call her up then!" And Feng then reached for his phone, on an old table and called. And Nia answering agreed, and tells them, to come pick her up at the house. And when they had arrived at her house, she was changing her clothes.

Chapter 9

Now, later that evening, Lloyd was parked one block away Howard Ave. And he, seated in the squad car, begins to call Renee. And she receives the call, going through her closet answering, "Hey... I was waiting for your call." He smiled and asked, "Hey, how is everything?... Sorry, I've been busy with work." Renee then held up a blue shirt, and placed it on the bed answers, "Everything is fine... I still can't believe I gave a cop my number... You're too cute in your uniform." And he laughed at the comment and asked, "Are you doing anything tonight?" She then sat on the bed answering, "Nothing at all, what are your plans?"

Lloyd immediately saw two cars pass by, and parked further down. And within seconds, he saw a group of guys come out, and begin to walk toward Howard Ave. And he found it to be suspicious said, "I'll call you right back." Renee in concern replies, "Hello!... Lloyd!?" Now, Alex was among the group, was looking around at the time. And Lloyd then got out of the squad car, and stood in the middle of the street watching. Now, Hill patrolling, had saw a cop looking straight down, and thought it was odd. And he immediately stomped on the brakes, and made a turn into the one-way street. And he saw an empty parking space, and parked behind him. Hill, now recognizing it was his partner with the window down says, "Evening, Lloyd." Now, Lloyd had met with him answering," Evening, Hill... Listen! Watch that crowd! Something's not right !" Hill then winks and says," I see them, I think we should radio it in... I've seen all but one before." And Lloyd looking back at the group says, "Let's wait and see... alright." Hill agreeing with him, started a new conversation says, "Alright... By the way..... have you had the coffee at the gas station on Lane Ave?... I've noticed you took the new squad car out. You should had told me as your partner, man!" And he laughed at the comment and says," Stay focused Hill, and no. I haven't had the coffee... But, I do find it funny, meeting you here... How's your wife?" Hill laughs and answered," She's fine, but was upset with me... We showed up late to her sister's wedding today... Anyways, the chief knew you'd be here... So, I came to check up on you... We all know you don't respond to any police text messages, just the ladies." And Lloyd ignored the remark, and watched the group again.

And the officers, seeing Alex for the first time, kept him in mind. Now, Richie wearing a hoodie and shades was beside Alex. And Alex within a few minutes, heard a car coming, had glanced back. And after seeing the cop car out of nervousness, says, "Great! The cops... Are they always around here?" Richie smirking at the comment replies, "Let them pass, who cares." And Alex panicing, says, "I do, I just hope it's worth it." Now, Richie then comforted him by saying, "Steve got you back, bro... Don't worry." Now, Hill then passed by viewing the crew, and left the street. And Lloyd had sat back in the squad car, in thought of Renee. And he later called back, to ask her to spend the night with him, and she agreed to come.

And the crew finally arrived walking behind a barbershop, and saw two white luxurious sport cars. And the cars were parked side by side, with four beautiful women conversating. And the wine store was further down the road. And Steve had saw Alex, and got out of the car to the left. And he embraces him with a hug, now curious about his presents. And Steve asked, "So, you decided to hang out or what's up?" And he answers," Getting more involved like you said... There was no parking space nearby... And we had to walk, all the way down here... Sucks." Steve laughs and says, "The guys that were with you, will protect you. I know everything in this town... These guys you see around me are my eyes." Now, Richie had laughed at the remark standing close by. And Steve then dismissed the crew, leaving them with the women. Now, Alex, feeling disturbed about his sister, based on his new lifestyle said, "Promise me, nothing will happen to Nia!?" And he assuring Alex, answered, "I promise, walk with me."

They then came to an alley and talked for an hour. And he had exposed his human trafficking plan to Alex only. And he felt that his cousin was perfect for the job. Now, Steve then made him swear, not to tell a soul or face death. And he agreed, and swore not to tell anyone. And Steve began to stare at him, to judge his trust and fate. And he hugged Alex, and says," Come, lets enjoy ourselves." And he didn't believe Alex, and was willing to kill him to keep order. And they came, and relaxed with the women for the evening.

And at that same hour, Feng, Nia and Angel had come late to the house party. And drinks were being served, and the music was loud and pumping. And Angel's girlfriend Amanda, was with her friend named Jasmine. And they were talking near the steps, and watching everything. Now, Jasmine, a crew member that was into Richie, were friends with benefits. Amanda had seen Angel enter in, and told Jasmine. Now, Jasmine had never seen Angel before, but heard her mention him. And she seen him for the first time, entered with company, asking about his friends. And Amanda, being unfamiliar with them, had shrugged her shoulders, giving no answer.

And when they walk through the crowd to the living room, Feng asks, "How'd you know about this party?" Angel answers, "It's my girlfriends, friend's party... And her name is Jasmine." Now, Angel had looked at Nia, and notice that she was being to herself asks, "Nia, you good?" She responds, "I'm fine." Now, Nia, not having any space to herself, felt uncomfortable. And she didn't want to be touched by the crowd, and was. So, she glanced at Feng becoming irritated, says, "I'll be outside." And she immediately headed outside. And he saw, and glanced at Feng asking, "Feng, Is she good?" He nodded yes, watching everything. Now, Angel then turns his attention elsewhere, looking at all the women. And he stared at a beautiful woman dancing near the kitchen. And he smirk, says, "Check the girl dancing near the kitchen, bro!" Feng avoided looking, instead he listened to the music being played. Now, Feng, not seeing Angel's girlfriend asked," Where Amanda at, bro?" And Angel had shrug at the comment, taking advantage of her absents. Now, Two women in the kitchen, had been watching them at the time. And they saw Nia and didn't care, and thought the fellas were cute. And they decided to approach them smiling, dressed in tight outfits. And the ladies had met with them, and one introduced herself saying, "Hi, my name is Roxy... And, this is my friend Becky." And Angel, with lusting eyes responds, "Hi, I am Angel and this is..." Feng interrupts, with an attitude said's, "Don't even!" And looks away.

Now, Nia then comes inside again, and sees the ladies flirting with them. And she feeling disrespected, had come over asking, "Ladies, can I help you with something?" And the ladies had gotten unset with the remark. And Angel had gotten upset with her given an attitude. Now, Roxy then frowned, and with an attitude answers," What?... Whatever, let's go Becky!" And they walked away, not liking her. Now, Feng then walked up to her, and outta of comfort, says, "It was nothing, you, ok?" She a bit annoyed answers, "No, let's go... I'm not feeling this party, Angel... Maybe next time, alright?" Now, Angel, watching them leave says, "You 've only been here for fifteen minutes!" And Feng shrugged his shoulders, and answers, "I got to go... I hope you and Amanda have a good time, bro!" Now, Nia, wondering who they were talking about, had stopped and asked, "Who's Amanda?" And he answered," His new girlfriend." And Angel heard, and got upset with her knowing! And they left, headed to his house for the evening. Now, Amanda then came to him, from behind asking," Angel, who were your friends? And Angel had turned around, becoming curious answered," That's Feng, my friend... And, his girl Nia Yung... Why?" Amanda says," Jasmine would like to know who her guest were... I'll tell her." And Angel, watching her leave, loudly said," HOW ABOUT YOU TELL ME WHERE YOU BEEN? And Amanda ignores him, and meets with Jasmine to gossip. And when Jasmine heard the last name Yung, she thought of Alex. And she later called Richie that evening.

Now, Lugo was home in bed that evening in thought of the case. And he then received a call from Chi. And he recognized the number with the phone near answers," Hello?" Chi then spoke with him about a very important meeting. And that he needed to be at the wine store tomorrow. And after the phone call, he felt that this should be the end of the case. Lugo then, was ready to give a report the next day.

Feng the next morning asleep, had dreamt about him and Lo. And they were talking outside a church, with the deacons behind them. And Lo asked, "So, you want to go to college to become an IT guy?" And he nodded yes, and says, "Yes... You know, I thank you for helping me become a good man... Nothing gangster, you know." Now, Lo thought the remark was odd, responds, "Why would you or anyone else, want that kind of life?... It's no way to raise a family." And Feng nodded again, answered, "I hear you pop." And after a few steps, Lo had said," Be ye separated, Second Corinthians six verse seventeen!"

Now, Feng then woke up to the phone ringing. And he had reached for the phone on the bed dresser. And after rubbing his eyes, he saw it was Lloyd. And he had removed the blanket from himself, watching Nia sleep. Now, Feng, seated on his side of the bed, softly answered, "What's up, Lloyd." And Lloyd answers, "I got to talk to you about something important big guy... Are you home?" And he became confused answers, "You're a cop, bro? I ain't got no bad news... Wait?" Feng after yawning, had realized the sun was out. And he saw the time, and continues saying," It's only seven in the morning, bro!... It ain't that serious..." Now, Lloyd hurried up, says, "It's about Nia's brother, I'm outside your house." He then hung up. Now, Feng then puts the phone back. And worried, bare chested in pajama pants. And he got up, and grabbed a t shirt from the dresser to put on. And Feng, in his slippers, had walked downstairs and came outside.

And he closed the door and saw Lloyd with photos standing near the porch. He then approached him asking, "What's up?... And how did you know where I live?" And Lloyd answers, "You're talking to a cop, remember... Listen, my partner and I had witnessed your girlfriend's brother at Howard Ave... And he was seen, hanging with a boss named, Steve Liang." Now, Feng in concern asked, "Did he kill anyone, wait?... How do you know I have girlfriend, and her brother?... And, who is Steve Liang?" And the officer then paused, and answers, "I don't want you involved, we go way back... There's an undercover cop involved... Come to found out Steve, and Alex are cousins... And you're dating or sleeping with the sister... Is that her car parked in front?" And Feng, feeling disappointed, had looked at her car, given no answer. And the officer then hands Feng the photos of Alex, with Nia loading groceries. And the photos included, Feng and Nia in his car. And another photo shows her car and licenses plate. And after he saw the photos, he gotten upset saying, "Lloyd, you messed up my whole morning, bro!... So, what now? Feng, giving it some thought says," That can't be the reason, she hasn't told her brother about me?" Now, Lloyd received the photos back, shrugs his shoulders. And he says, "I'd kill the relationship thing, don't get involved or close!... I don't wanna lose a friend." Now, Lloyd then embraced him with a handshake and walked away. And Feng being sarcastic replies, "Don't get involved?... Thanks, Lloyd!" Feng then shouts," YOU KNOW, I HAVE AN ANNIVERSARY COMING UP!" And Lloyd turned around, says," My question to you is... Why doesn't Alex know about you?... You said he doesn't know about you, right?... I got to go." Now, Feng thought about the comment watching him leave.

Now, later that day, Nia came home. And she parked in front, not seeing her brother's car. And she was hoping he was there, to talk about her relationship. And she had opened the door, and was left clueless as to where he could be. Now, Alex at the time, was with Richie, Steve and four women hanging out. And they were outside the parking lot of the warehouse he lived in. Now, Alex's phone on the car seat, had received a call. And Richie nearby, heard the phone says, "Alex, your phone!" And he stops conversating with a woman, and saw it was Nia. And he had ignored the call, and met with the lady again. Now, Steve saw, and in concern had asks, "Who is it?" And he answers, "It's my sister, it's nothing." And Steve nodded, and continued talking with the girls around him. And Nia, getting no answer, had sat the phone on the passenger seat. And she then opened, and closed the glove compartment for photos of her with Feng. And she sat the photos next to her phone, closing the door. And she, reflecting on Feng's behavior this morning, had thought it was very awkward. And left the matter alone, and drove to clear her head for a bit.

Lloyd later that afternoon was off duty, and on the phone with Renee. And he, being ready to leave, stood near his car, had saw how busy the plaza was. And he at the time, was across the street from a busy ice cream store. And had no idea he was being followed by a crew member named Danny. Now, Danny was a regular crew member, that hated him for patrolling in their area. And he was walking slowly among the people, and saw an opportunity to kill him. And he, without orders, had gotten a woman's attention coming outside a store. And had paid her $100 dollars to draw his attention close to the ice cream store for a surprise. And he, lying to her, said that they were friends. And the lady thought it was odd, but agreed, not knowing his intentions. And had walked off. And he then walked away, and hid in between cars. And he watched her walk down to the store, reaching for a gun from behind the waist.

Now, Renee in a flirting manner asked, "Can we pick up where we had left off? "And she at the time, was walking around the living room bored. And Lloyd smiled and answered, "Yeah!... What are you doing?... I'm off duty right now." Renee then puts her hair in a bun. And she, still in a flirtatious manner responds, "You mean wearing!... How fast can you get here?... I want to see you !" And he sat on the hood of his car, says, "Wow!... I don't know what to say to that !... I'm ten minutes from you, what are you wearing?" She answers, "I'm wearing a large jersey of your favorite team!" And she was walking to the bedroom to lay down. And Lloyd then reached for his keys, and stood straight up. Now, the lady near the ice cream store, had waved at him smiling. And Lloyd's attention was caught, and they made eye contact. And she, having his attention, had shouted for directions. Now, Lloyd saw, and thought it was awkward. And he had met with her asking,"

What's that?" Now, Danny saw, and stood up, taking aim. And he with an evil grin, starts to shoot at Lloyd from a distance. And the people near the store immediately scattered. And Lloyd had gotten hit in the arm, and back. And the lady facing him was in shock, and started to scream running inside the store. And the store manager saw, and begun to hide behind the register. And the customers were on the ground panicking. And Lloyd in pain, had ran back to the car dropping the phone nearby. And he, now reached for his gun at the waist, saw and took aim. And he realized, the shooting angle beside them would be tough. And the people around the area, hid and screamed. Now Lloyd, being shielded by his car, begins to glance over shouts, "YOU WANT THIS!!... YOU WANT ME!!" And he fired back at Danny. Now, Renee at the time, heard the shooting, had stood up. And she immediately worried about him, shouts, "OH MY GOD!... OH MY GOD! LLOYD!!... OH MY GOD!!" And a squad car at the time, had speeds around the corner with the sirens on. And Danny fires off two shots around Lloyd's area. And he, not seeing Lloyd, had run to his car and quickly drove off. Now, Lloyd seen the cop car enter the plaza, and stop in front of him. And two officers came out of the car to his aid. And he, without his phone, had asked for it. And one officer watching him point in the direction had seen it, and gave it to him. Now, Lloyd, being in pain, had texted Lugo. And the people near, had risen and gathered around in shock. And the lady paid by Danny, felt bad for Lloyd. She didn't know that this would lead to violence. And she and the store manager had come to the police, and told them what had happened. And indeed, this made the news.

    Nia at that same hour, was in her car parked. And she was deep in thought outside Feng's house. And she was having a flash back, of the first time she met Lo. Now, this took place at a park, early in the afternoon. And Lo hadn't seen Feng in two days, and sat on a bench worried, viewing an empty parking lot. And he needed to be in a place of peace, before calling the cops. So, he had meditated on scriptures of peace, to ease his mind. And his attention, was soon caught by a car that had entered in. And he, from a distance, saw a car that looked very familiar come near. And the car then parked near the bench, and Feng came out. And he, wanting to surprise his father, asked," Dad, how are you?" Lo then stood up and frowned at him. And in a worried, and demanding voice he says, "I'm good… Listen, where were you?… I haven't seen you in two days!" Feng met with him says, "Dad, I met someone…. Why are you alone in the park?… Were you meditating?" Now, Lo calming down, had become curious says, "I'm always alone in the park meditating on peace, you know this… Who?" Nia then got out of the car and met with them. And he, looking at Feng asks, "Is she the one?" And Feng nodded yes, and answers, "Yes, it's her." She then greeted him says," Hi, I'm Feng girlfriend… Nia Yung." And Lo looked at them, and smiled saying, "What a cute couple… I'll tell your mother!" Now, Lo, still in remembrance of his absents says ,"…. Don't run off like that again, Feng… I almost, called the cops." And he knew his father was worried answers, "Sorry, I won't!"

And Nia came out the flash back, locking the car door. And she shows up, opening the front door of the house.

Now, Feng was waiting in the living room, pacing back and forth with the TV on. And he then turns the TV off, hearing the door closed. And she came into the living room, and saw him deep in thought. He then looked at her with a serious attitude. And he met with her saying, "We need to talk." Now, Nia feeling confused asked, "Talk about what?… What's wrong, babe?" He answers, "I don't know how else to say it." Now, Nia immediately shouts, "JUST SAY IT, IS IT THAT GIRL THAT WAS AT THE PARTY?… ARE YOU LEAVING ME?"

Feng says "Nia, it's your brother Alex." And she answers, "My brother?... What about my brother!" She now, raising her voice again, had asked, "WHAT ABOUT MY BROTHER!?... WHAT DID YOU DO?" He asked," Do?... I didn't do anything." Now, she gets in his face, asking, "What did you say?... Talk to me!!" Feng responds, "I didn't say anything... Your brother doesn't know we're dating!... Let alone, I've never been inside your house!" She answers," My brother wouldn't like you... If he knew we were together, he'd make problems for you... He did it with my last relationship... And I apologize for not inviting you in the house, Feng." Now, Feng then took a breather, and response, "Aside from you hiding me from your brother... Alex is being watched by the cops... He's rocking with some thugs downtown on Howard Ave." Now, Nia in concern for her brother shouts, "IS YOUR COP FREIND WATCHING MY BROTHER!?... FENG? .... IS THIS COP WATCHING MY BROTHER!?" He loudly answered, "YES!... THE COPS ARE WATCHING HIS INVOLVEMENT WITH THE GANG!" Now, Tears started to stream down her cheek, and she felt he was being disloyal. And Nia calming down, had backed away says, "Feng... He's, my brother. My family, you understand!... If you are going to be with me, then be with me!... Tomorrow is going to be our anniversary." And Feng then shook his head no, and says, "Yeah, I understand... Pack your stuff and leave!" Now, Nia in shock asked, "Feng !... Why?" And he in a serious manner responds, "The danger, and hiding our relationship!... Leave !... Get out!" And Feng had points at the door, watching her. And Nia, with tears, had left the house upset. And she knew then that the secret was out.

And an hour later, Lewis was seated in his office frustrated with Hill. And they were in discussion about the situation with Lloyd. Lugo then showed up to give a report, closing the door says," Hey, I've some news... Sorry, I couldn't get here sooner... Chi wanted to see me." And Lewis out of frustration says, "Somebody please explain to me, what is going on here?... Officer Lloyd, is in the hospital right now, why?" Lugo answers, "His name is Danny... He's a cocky fella in the gang... Lloyd had described him to me, shortly after by text." And the sergeant replies in a sarcastic manner, "Cocky?... You're telling me."

Lugo said, "In Lloyd's case... Danny doesn't like him." Now, Lewis then turns his attention to Hill asking," Officer Hill, do you have anything for me?" And he responds, "No, sir!" Lewis then glanced at his deck asking," I have an officer shot twice... Detective, should I move now?" And he answers," No.... Chi had called me last night... Today he called, and wanted me to meet him at the wine store. And he wanted to make sure I understood again in fact.... Steve is having a meeting with mobsters. And this mob owns two-gun shops in the state of Indiana, trafficking illegal guns... Steve's plan is to get the weapons, and a face lift surgery... He wants to leave the country clean, and rich with the crew. Chi said that we will know the location soon; it could be the U. K, you know." Now, Lugo, given the ladies involved with the crew some thought says,"... The four ladies that sleep with the crew, should now be questioned... And they can be found at a club on 77 Ave called Lollykiss... Or the Yogurt Store on Brim Street. That's on the other side of town... Terry has everyone's name and photo on the chart... That's all I have." And the sergeant wanting more details, regarding the guns asked,"... And how is he going to hide all of those guns out the country, detective?" He answers," I don't know yet... I don't even know where out of the country, remember... I'll get the date and address... Everyone will be there from my understanding... It's going to be big, boss... Give me time, I need time." Now, Lewis had stared at him very sternly, and answered, "You find out! And you tell me, Lugo!... And I'll send the other detectives to question these women." He nodded and answered, "Yes sir!" Lewis in thought says, 'Receiving guns out of state, there's something to that." He then paged Mary and Peter. And they came to the office, leaving the door open and were told what to do next. And the sergeant wanted the arrest made, concerning the owners of the gas stations. He knew now was the right time.

Now, Monty the chief of police, had showed up to the office with three men from the F. B. I. And Lewis stood up a bit confused asking," Monty, what's going on?" Monty disappointed says," Sergeant, this is F. B. I Reginal director Mick Mercer... To your right is special agent Tod, with special agent Jon. "Lewis then told Hill to close the door. And he, coming to the door, had seen Linda the bartender with her boyfriend. And he closed the door shut, and faced them." Now, Mick says, "This case is our case regarding Mr. Liang. Anything organized crime or drug related, we step in... In short, I am asking you not to get involved." And Lewis, arguably spoke up, saying," We've been after Liang for some time now... Where we you?" And Mick smirked, and answers ," Do you really think you were the only ones watching him.... Your now in our way, and again this is our case... Mrs. Miles is now in the witness protection with us... We found her going to the door of her apartment in South Carolina." Now, Lewis being sarcastic says, "I see... You didn't think we'd get this far, director!" And they continued to argue for five minutes and agreed to disagree. And the two detectives later that day, have been watching for the ladies on Brim Street. And the ladies never showed up.

Chapter 10

Now, three days later in the morning, Lloyd was resting in a recovery room in the hospital accompanied by Renee. And she, slowly rubbed his shoulder says, "I'm glad, you're ok." Now, Lloyd in thought of Feng replies, "Do me a favor and call this number... My phone is charging." And Feng at the time, was driving and received a call. And he saw an unfamiliar number answered, "What's up?... Who's this?" He then pulled in front of a bakery and heard Lloyd's voice in concern.

Lugo at the time, was coming out of the bakery with a bag of pastries and saw him. And he quickly walked behind him, crossing the street to his car. Now, Lugo, using his keys, had opened the door. And he placed the bag on the passenger seat and heard a car come. And he saw Richie passing by and was surprised. Now, Richie then made a right turn, entering an alley behind an old building. And Lugo became curious and remembered to look for clues. And he had recognized the store from across. And he thought to himself, that this is where Steve is hiding. And he closed the door, and walked over to the building. And he peeked, and saw Steve greeting Richie by the car. And he immediately walked back to his car and didn't see Feng. And he drove to the police department to give a report.

Later that day, Steve had seen Danny on the news and was disappointed. So, he texted him for a one on one. And Danny, receiving the address was driving near at the time. And he thought about the meet up, and was clueless to the news.

10 minutes later, Danny arrived at a warehouse he's never been to before. And he entered in and was brought to the office by the armed guard. Now, Steve stood near the desk, watching him stop at the desk. And he with a serious look says, "You know I know, right?... In that plaza, there were lots of cameras." And the thought then hit Danny, as he begins to look down ashamed. And he, wanting to explain himself answers, "Sorry, Lord... The cop on the news, stays in our neighborhood." Now, Steve slowly takes a seat, says, "I didn't give you the order, Danny. And because he's a cop, and you missed.... It's dangerous that you live." And he gave the ok for the guard to kill him. And the guard then came to him from behind, and he began to panic. And the guard stood at 6 feet 3, and weight 260 pounds, reaching for his shirt. And the guard began to grab and drag him from behind, hearing him shouts, "BUT, WAIT!!... WAIT!!" And Steve at the time, was brainstorming how to quiet the whole situation. And he continued to hear him cry out for mercy, and tried to focus.

Feng that same hour, had arrived at the hospital to meet with Lloyd. And he came in the room worried asking, "Are you ok?... The doctor says, you took one in the back, and another in the arm." And Lloyd in pain answered, "Yeah." He then introduced Renee to him says,"... Feng, this is Renee." And she then greets Feng asking, "Hi, Feng... Are you a cop?" Lloyd answered, "We're just friends, we grew up together." And she says to Feng," That's a beautiful name for an American." Now, Lloyd, wanting a word in private with Feng asked, "Can you give us a minute?" And Renee said, "Sure, sure." And she grabbed her purse, and left the room. And Lloyd saw and says, "Feng, be careful... Those thugs were on to me... And, if you're still involved with the sister... Well." And he paused, and goes on to say, "I remember, what the guy that aimed at me looks like." Now, Feng, in thought of her responds," Nia and I had broken up last night... It's over." Lloyd smiled, saying, "Good man, good man. You go in peace... I'm looking forward to the police raid on Howard Ave... The detective is giving us a lot." And Feng says, "Sounds like this will be over soon enough." And he understood the warning and left.

Renee then came back chewing candy asked," Is everything alright?" And he nodded yes, watching her take a seat. And she then had a sour taste in her mouth, and saw the bathroom said," I'll be right back." And when she went into the bathroom, closing the door, a nurse had come into the room. Now, Lloyd's phone near the bathroom, had received a text message. And he asks the nurse for the phone. And when he received it, he saw a message from Vicky. Now, Vicky looked like a beautiful Greek model, at 6 feet 1, with dark curly hair and blue eyes. And the message had mentioned how much she missed him, and wanted to come and visit tomorrow morning. Now, Lloyd, out of lust had smiled, and text back please do. And she lastly text, shake my tree or get no peaches. And he laughs at the comment, knowing what she meant. And he then receives a text message out of nowhere from Anne, saying hello stranger. Now, Anne looked like a very attractive hipster, slim and short, with a Spanish ascent. And she mentioned that she is no longer with Tylor, and wants him at her place, like it used to be. And Renee then came out of the restroom, and saw the nurse leaving. And he turned the phone off, watching her take a seat. And he lied, knowing she had saw the phone said," It was my mother." And they smile, and joined hands. And they enjoyed each other's company, til she left.

Now, that same hour, Nia had argued with Alex in the living room. And he annoyed shouts, "NIA, IT DOSEN'T MATTER

THAT I AM WITH STEVE!... HE UNDERSTANDS FAMILY!" And she shouts back, "STOP THIS, YOU KNOW BETTER!... I DON'T WANT YOU TO GO TO JAIL!" And Alex says, "Oh, stop!... Steve, doesn't kill at all!" He then receives a call from Richie. And he reached into the back pocket and answered. And Nia had walked away, frustrated into the dining room. And he says, "Yeah?" And Richie asked, "Is your sister seeing somebody?" Now, Alex giving his full attention answered, "No, why?" He says," Word is, your sister came to my girl's party with a date... Lord Liang, wants to know who he is... Find out, bro." Alex responds "Alright." Richie then hangs up. And he slowly puts his phone down, on the living room table.

And when she saw that he was off the phone, she returned to the living room. Now, she becomes curious asked, "What's up?" And he then met with her asking, "Do you have a boyfriend?" And she feeling awkward answers," No, I don't. Why is it important, Alex?... and who's asking?" And he answers, "You were being watched at a party!... What's his name, if he's not your boyfriend?" Now, she avoiding eye contact, answered, "Feng... Some guy I met." And Alex feeling puzzled, then recognized the name responds, "Wait!... Pastor Lo Feng's, son?... I remember seeing him, passing by a service." And she answered, lying with a fake laugh," Yes, it was nothing!" Now, Alex understood and says, "I'll tell Steve it was nothing." And she, being in concern for Feng asked, "You're not going to kill him or anything?" Now, Alex noticing her behavior asked, "Nia?... Who is he, to you?" And she lied again, answering," Nothing!... He's nothing." Now, she goes back into the dining room, and stood worried for Feng. And he, watching her says, "We'll see... Come with me tomorrow... I want to talk with him." And she faced him, answered, "Alright." Alex then nodded, and left the house to clear his head. And Nia then had a bad feeling about this whole situation, and began to pray.

She knew, she needed to warn Feng in person. And she begins to gather her thoughts, and within seconds had prayed. And she with all her heart says, "Lord Jesus, take away the hurt in my family, and protect Feng... In Jesus name, Amen."

Now, Nia later that night, was in her bed asleep. And she was dreaming, back when she was nine years old. About the time her father was anger with her, over the low school grades. And he had pushed her up against the wall, in the living room shouting, "HOW STUPID ARE YOU!... YOUR JUST LIKE YOUR MOTHER, WITH NO BRAINS!... NOW, GO TO YOUR ROOM... AND STUDY UNTIL I TELL YOU TO STOP!... DO YOU HEAR ME ?!" Nia crying, loudly says, "YES!" And ran to her room. Now, Nia, still dreaming, had turned to the other side sleeping. And Alex at the time, had shown up at her door.

And he took advantage of his sister sleeping, opening the door quietly. And he saw her purse on the dresser, and took it. He then opened it, and saw a photo of her kissing Feng. And he, in search, had found a recent picture of them. And he felt disappointed closing her purse, and sat it back. And he, with the photos, had closed the door back quietly. And wanted to address the issue in the morning.

The next morning, at downtown New Haven around 6:40 a.m. The garbage men had come around for the trash. And a new garbage man had started that day. And he, being new, had become curious about the trash. And he wanted to judge how light the bags were, to avoid the heavy lifting. And when they came to blue street on a normal run. He saw and touched a bag among a few, near a dump shaped differently. And he immediately called his coworkers' attention to come near. And the three of them gathered, and one said to their senior, open it. And the senior garbage man knew that they looked up to him to investigate. And he, being encouraged, had opened it. And they then witnessed, a body with blood around the ribs. And the body had no head, but the head was in the bag. And the trash men, had quickly moved away in disgust. The driver then called 911.

15 minutes later the police arrived, and were told everything by the garbage men. Detective Peter and Mary were there, and came near the body. And they saw stab wounds on the right rib. And the face had one black eye, and an odor due to the head being unattached. And the detectives knew that this had to be an act of punishment, due to his last appearance. And the street was indeed closed by the police. And the body was identified as Danny, and it made the news.

Renee that morning, had come to the hospital to see Lloyd again. And a new nurse had saw her waiting, to be checked in, at the front desk asked, "Ma'am, who are you looking for?" And she answered, "Lloyd, Lloyd Chase." And the nurse thought it was odd, remembering him checkout, says, "I believe he checked out already with a skinny lady, with red hair... A young lady." She then frowned, not understanding why said, "Thanks, Ma'am." And she felt disappointed leaving the hospital. And the nurse saw and began to worry about her. And the usual front desk nurse heard, walking back to the station. And she met with the nurse, and saw Renee leave said," That lady was here yesterday... So, I don't know what's going on." And they went back to work.

Now, Lloyd at the time, was home in the bedroom talking with his ex-girlfriend named, "Vicky." And his thoughts were, to have her leave early, to avoid being caught. And Renee, within minutes, was about to arrive at his house. Now, he then sat on the bed, and received a call from Lugo. And Lloyd, with the phone at the foot of the bed answered, "Hello." Now, Lugo, parked in front of a corner store says, "Lloyd !... Listen, Steve is about to receive illegal weapons." Now, Vicky immediately got up, and went to the bathroom wearing his hockey jersey. And he saw and asked

"When?" And Lugo answers, "This evening... Also, the guy that tried to kill you, was found dead... Steve, had him killed so that's that... And I was fortunate to shopped for pastries and saw Steve with Richie... Steve's hideout spot... So, we now know that Shogun Ave is where he stays... Who knew, it be at across from a cheap store downtown New Haven... And by the way, Lewis doesn't want you at the raid... Not to mention, the F. B. I is now involved... Not that you could come anyhow." Now, Lloyd in thought answers, "Wait the F. B. I?... Where, and why guns? Thanks for telling me, I won't get involved." And Lugo looking around responds, "Yes, there now involved... The guns are coming from a gun shop run by a mob, in the state of Indiana... He's meeting at an old warehouse on 58 Gardens Ave... And why guns, to kill I guest... Rest well man, bye."

Now, Vicky then came out of the bathroom, putting her hair into a ponytail. And Lloyd in thought said, "Alright." And he hung up, and threw the phone back on the bed. And she sat with him, and they began to kiss. Now, Vicky was very excited to have him said," I wanna cook you breakfast." And he, wanting her to leave answered," Let's do a beautiful thing next time hun, okay?" And she became curious asked," Why?" And they heard the doorbell ring. And she saw him reach for his phone asked," Who's that?" And they got up, and made their way downstairs. And he came to the front door and saw Renee through the square glass. And she had waited for him to open the door, looking at an unfamiliar car parked out front, with her arms crossed. And Lloyd didn't know what to say to her. Now, Renee being impatient, shouts, "WHY! WHY LLOYD!... THE NURSE HAD TOLD ME THAT YOU LEFT THE HOSPITAL WITH A RED HEADED BIMBO! ...... ARE YOU GONNA EVEN OPEN THE DOOR?!" Now, Lloyd had opened the door ashamed. And Vicky, wanting no parts, went into the kitchen. Now, Lloyd, in a soft tune voice says, "Renee,

Renee... I'm sorry." And she looked at him, and saw his ex with a long jersey in disgust. And she, hurt by the situation, says, "And I thought you were different from the other jerks I've dated." And he had reached for her hand, and she moved it. And she says," Lose my number, we're done!" Lloyd then watched her leave, knowing he was wrong. And Vicky went into the refrigerator with an attitude asking," Lloyd! Who was that?... And who was she calling a bimbo?" And he closed the door answering," Some sales lady!... She wasn't taking about you, hun... Still wanna cook me breakfast?" And she smiled, and reached into the breakfast pantry to make breakfast for them.

And that afternoon, Alex was home on the phone with Steve about Feng. And Steve pacing around his desk had asked, "So, what are you saying?" Alex said, "Nia has or had a lover, and his name was Feng... I don't know why she hid him from me? I know of him, and his father... And I don't like Lo Feng, with all that bible stuff." Now, Steve frowned saying," Because she doesn't want you to know, it sounds like trouble. And I cannot have trouble, Alex!... I'll send Lugo to deal with him!" And Steve took a seat thinking about the whole situation. And Alex replies, "Steve, I'll handle it!" And Steve thought it was odd, and wanted a reassurance asked, "... You're going to kill him? Have you ever used a gun before?" Alex thought about it and answered," Yes. No, never used a gun before... Don't give the order to Lugo." Now, Steve ready to hang up said," I'll send you help, alright?... This man is a danger in my eyes." And Alex, with a question in mind quickly asked," Hey. Question, when I said yes and joined... You, me and a few of the crew that day in your office... Why did Lucky have a bible, and was reading Deuteronomy 28 verse 15 and down." And Steve laugh and answers," Curses, you mean?... Because I want you, and everyone else to see me as your lord... Understand. "Now, Alex, not liking the whole idea, knew he was in too deep says," I understand." And Alex, in thought of Jasmine says,"... So, Jasmine will be on the search for young girls for the investor, right?" Steve answers," After I give the order, yes... I'll see you tonight at 58 Gardens Ave." And Steve hung up. And Alex too, looking at the photos again on the living room table. And he showed up at her door, moving the knob around, and couldn't get in. And he had called out her name, and heard nothing. And he, being upset, had called her phone and received no answer. And he then leaves the house wondering where she could be.

And Nia indeed left early in the morning to avoid her brother. And aside from Feng's protection, she knew that she needed to move away.

And Feng later that afternoon, receives a phone call from Nia while driving. Now, she was parked in a busy plaza wearing dark shades, waiting for him to respond. And he, recognizing the number answered, "Hello?" Now, Nia looking around, urgently responds, "Feng!... Listen, my brother is looking for you... I don't know what his intentions are, but it's not good!" And Feng, wanting to better understand her message, saw an empty parking space nearby and parked. And he thought it strange, had asked, "Nia, what are you talking about?... And why is he looking for me?... What did you tell him?" And she asked, "Where are you?... I will tell you in person." And he had looked at the avenue sign near answers, "I'm on Lex Ave, close to an old bar. "And she said, "Wait for me there." And he checking the area out said, "Alright." And he saw many vacant houses, and heard the subway from above.

And she drove to meet with Feng. And she, within minutes, had passed Alex in the other lane. And he seen her, and quickly made a U turn, almost causing an accident to follow. And he kept his distance, believing she was meeting Feng again.

Now, Lugo at the time, was seated with Steve in the back seat of a car. And they were headed to the usual vacant warehouse, for transactions on 58 Gardens Ave. Chi was driving with Lucky at the passenger seat. And Steve kept two briefcases filled with money in the trunk of the car. And the crew drove their cars in a straight line, Steve was in the back. Now, Lugo not seeing Richie had asked, "Where's Richie? And Steve smirks at the comment and answers, "I sent Richie to help Alex out. .... I need you to stay focus on what is about to happen now... We're going there early." And Lugo nodded in agreeance. So, the transaction and Feng's troubles were happening at the same time.

Now, Feng had seen her car from a distance, and got worried. And she had parked near him, and saw him on the phone. Now, Lloyd was in the kitchen at the time, and heard his phone on the counter ring. And he looked, and saw it was Feng. And Vicky was in her own world cooking. Lloyd answers, "Feng!... What's up?" And he asked, "Could you come down to Lex Ave, something isn't right... It's a police matter, bro." Now, Lloyd then thought to include his partner in, but doesn't due to pride. And he still feeling pain from his arm answered, "I'm on my way." And she saw him hang up asked," Where are you going?" And he kissed her, and answers," I gotta make a quick run!... I'll be back!" And she watched him open and close the door shaking his arm. And she was indeed clueless to the matter.

Now, Nia at the time, closed the car door and met with Feng. And he hung up, and got out of the car seeing another car pull up. And Alex had parked next to her car, with a frown. And he knew he had to prove his loyalty at any cost. Now, Feng had thrown the phone at the car seat asking," Nia, who is that?" She glanced, and knew it was her brother. And she knew that they never met before. And she, removed her shades, in shocked that he had found them. And Alex then texted Richie where he was, and that he was given the order to kill Feng. And he texted back, "Yeah, Steve just texted me... I'll be there in three minutes." And she then explains everything to Feng, and he gets upset. And Nia concerned says, "Feng, you need to hide. Leave the state or tell the police... I believe my brother wants to kill you!" And Feng arguably asked, "Why?... What did you tell him?" And she paused in great concern, and began answering, "We were seen at the party... And my brother was questioned about you... Like you don't understand, it's because he's in a gang now!" And she worried for his life, developing tears. And she then dropped her shades, and hugged him.

And he then understood said, "Alright... Alright, we'll go to the police." Now, Alex had got out the car with the photos shouting, "MY OWN SISTER!... IS HE A COP OR SOMETHING?... WHO IS HE?" Now, Richie then showed up, and parked behind Alex with two men. And Alex saw, and had met with them. And he then pointed at Feng during their conversation, and was handed a gun. Now, Feng then moves her aside close by. And she saw her brother, put the gun behind his waist. And she immediately shouts, "FENG, IS NOT A COP!... WHAT DO YOU WANT WITH HIM !?" Now, Alex had raised the photos of them saying, "We don't know him, and you hid him from me.... Nia that's dangerous!... Steve sent me to deal with him." And Feng then begins to cross his arms asking, "What do you mean deal with me?... You threatening me!?" Richie then met with Feng, and pulled out a knife. And he with a serious look, starts to attack him anywhere. And Feng had blocked the knife, quickly holding his arm. And he knocks him out with a punch to the face. Now, Alex had waved the men to attack him. And during the fight, he ran and grabbed his sister. And she begins to scream out for help. And the people in the bar heard, and came out worried. And Alex saw, and covered her mouth using his hand shouts," GO BACK INSIDE OR I'LL MAKE

YOU GO BACK !!" And the people, and the bar owner continued to watch, wanting no parts of the violence. But, in watching the unfairness, they looked to the owner to stop the fight. And the owner didn't know what to think. Now, Alex, watching Feng fight back shouts," BEAT HIM DOWN FIRST!... AND, I'LL FINISH HIM OFF!" And Nia witnessed the fight of two martial artists against one, and was worried for feng.

Meanwhile at 58 Gardens, Steve and his crew with the money had arrived and came to the entry door. And the crew all seen two mob guards, and looked at Steve. And he took notice of how early the mob was, and was ready himself. And when asked, he told the guards who he was. And he became a little worried, that things could go wrong, watching one guard call their boss, and was given the okay to enter. And they then went inside a one floor warehouse, passing another guard near the hallway with many rooms. And they opened another door, leading to another hallway. And they came to the last door into the area, where the mob was. And with no power, the transaction needed to be quick. And the crew saw a table with two wooden crates, assuming the guns were in it. Now, Steve, not trusting Larry the mob boss, with four men around said, "I see your twenty minutes early... I'm Lord Liang, Open the crates." And Larry also with trust issues, answers, "Money first, let's make this fast." And this being the first time that they met, they wanted the transaction to be smooth. Now, Steve gave the okay to Chi by nodding yes. And he walked over to the table and met with Larry. And he had seen the money and felt relieved. And he asked," So, you want me to take care of the guns and airport situation, right? "Steve nodded yes and said," I can't be seen around here... I must be a ghost, my boys too... Thanks." Now, Larry then told, one of his men to show the guns. And he had glanced at the crew saying," Don't thank me, thank your brother... God rest his soul for searching us out." And Steve looking around says," The Mayor will be killed tomorrow... This city needs to be reminded, who the real Principality in the flesh is. "And Larry then smirks at the comment.

And the police at the time, were parked in three vans among cars, less than a block away. And three cops were dressed like civilians, watching the two guards at the door. And the guards seem unarmed and focused. Now, Terry was parked near in a van, watching the warehouse by screen. And Lewis in the van, among the officers, had held the door ready says, "Wait for my signal!" Now, there was another squad parked, waiting with a two blocks radius. And everyone was waited patiently, for the signal.

Now, Peter and Mary at that same exact time, had seen a car parked in front of the yogurt store. And the detectives, already parked, were hoping to catch one of the ladies that day. Mary had focused on her phone, and Peter was looking straight ahead out of boredom. And his partner asked ," Have you noticed that Lewis keeps assigning us here and there." And he answers," Yeah... But, everything seems to be connected from the gas station, to watching Steve's house, the shop and then some. "And he looked across out of curiosity, and recognized the driver's face. And he called his partner's name to gain her attention, viewing the photos between them says," The driver is our girl." And they seen the other girls coming out of the car, and were matching the photos. And the detectives, surprised, had recognized that these were the ladies, watching them go inside. And the detectives being across from them, had begun to move.

And the other officers were at the gas stations, arresting the owners at the time. And the arrest caused a crowd of people, recording with their phones. And the owners were indeed embarrassed, covering their faces. And said nothing without a lawyer .

Now, Steve at the time, was in a rush. And he, being impatient says, "Like you said, let's make this fast... It's been 10 minutes already." Lugo stood behind the crew armed, and saw everything. And he knew that now was the time, and softly spoken to the wire on his chest saying," Now!"

And Lewis heard through his radio earpiece, and gives the signal shouting, "GO! GO! GO!" And the police then came out of the vans, and began to raid the building. And the other squad begin to block the streets, now a block away, watching the warehouse. And the guards were caught off guard by the three officers near, having them at gun point. And the guards had quickly surrender, seeing the police come. And the guard at the entry door inside, had heard the cops, and ran to the mob shouting," THE POLICE ARE HERE !!" Now, Larry was caught off guard, and didn't trust the exchange, shouted, "YOU SET ME UP!" And Steve surprised, loudly argued back, "NO!... YOURE THE COP!" And the crew, and mob have their weapons drawn at each other. And Chi, wanting to avoid the mob and cops, had said," Boss, the back door is the only way out!... We gotta go!" And Larry then glanced at the back door saying," Steve, you ain't leaving here alive!" And the guard then waves at the mob, aiming the gun at the hall. And the crew had watched the mob, move slowly towards the back door. And the police with the two guards, had found guns behind their waist, and breached the front door. And the police were now inside, and within a few minutes, had seen the armed guard. And they went into the empty rooms for their safety. And the guard had opened fire until he ran out of bullets. And when he did, the shooting had stopped for about a minute. And the cops had judged that he was out of bullets, and rushed into the hallway shouting," FREEZE!... DROP YOUR WEAPONS!" And the guard in a panic mode was reloading, watching the mob come near the back door. And he glanced back and aimed, and was shot dead in the chest.

And the police then came in the main area surrounding everyone shouting, "FREEZE! DROP YOUR WEAPONS!" And more cops had come through the back door on guard. And everyone did what they were told, but Lugo. Now, the police had seen the two wooden crates of illegal guns, and the two briefcases, filled with one hundred thousand dollars in each. And the arrest was now being made. And one of the cops, had saw that the detective feeling relieved said," Good work, detective." And the crew, and mob, now understood how the raid had happened. Now, the F. B. I had showed up, and come inside. And the police and fed's didn't get along at all.

10 minutes later, the police had raided Steve's warehouse. And the guard outside, hearing the sirens, had called it in, but received no answer. And he thought to drive off, but knew it was too late. And the guard then saw the police cars rushing around, and he surrendered, unarmed with his hands up. And the guard, being approached by armed policemen, was now made to open the door. And the police then arrested the guard at the entry door, and one-armed guard surprised, in the hallway.

Now, Mia was seated in the office, on the phone with a friend, gossiping. And she glanced at the surveillance camera, and saw the police rushing inside. And she got up and panicked, hanging the phone up. And had reflected over her life, reaching into a drawer for a gun. And the police then showed up at the office door closed, and stood to the wall. And two officers near the door, had no idea what was going on in the room. And the officers had made eye contact, and agreed on the count to three to open. Now, Mia, in a sarcastic manner shouts," I WOULDNT OPEN THIS DOOR IF I WERE YOU!" And an officer, now reaching for the doorknob, shouts," MISS, WE ARE COMING IN!" And when the door opened, the officer aimed his gun at her. And he was also at gun point. And the officer, in a calmly manner had stood still, said," Freeze." And she, with a mean look, had opened fire around the desk, hitting the bulletproof vest. And she had used the chair as a shield, focusing on the officer. And the other officer immediately came in, moving away from the officer down. And the officer had fired two shots at her arm, and shoulder, watching her fall, releasing the gun. And the officer that was down, immediately got up armed. And he ran, and met with her aiming the gun shouted," FREEZE!" Now, Mia had raised her hands up, ready to get cuffed by him. And she saw the other officer approaching asked," Why didn't you finish me?" And the officer ignored the comment, putting the gun away. And she was now cuffed, and read her rights in an angry manner.

Peter, Mary and Lewis had met with the officers inside, and were told what had happened. And Lewis had thought, the detective's presents was kind of odd had, asked," I assume, you two have finally spoken with the girls?" And Peter answered," Yes... We met them at the yogurt store, boss. And they are down at the station now... Seeing we have them, we thought to come, and investigated here too." Now, Mary in remembrance, of the tasty yogurt says," The yogurt was on point too, boss." And the sergeant had chuckle and nodded, looking around. And the F. B. I had showed up, and agent Tod had met with Lewis. And he had harsh words with Lewis, over control of the case. And they agreed to disagree, believing that the case was over now. And the case later, became a joint task force. And the F. B. I wanted the police in court, to better close the case. And this was an act of giving credit to Lewis and Monty, the chief of police.

Now, Lloyd around that same time arrives, to help Feng. And he had parked near the old bar. And the people outside the bar had seen him. And he was away from the scene with a gun, waving his badge to the people. And he saw two guys attacking Feng, and Alex holding Nia. And he opened the door with a gun, coming to their defense. Now, Feng, blocking a kick, had forcefully thrown a guy to the other, against a parked car. And Alex then felt, he took Feng lightly. And he seen Lloyd armed and coming, and panicked, shouting," WATCH OUT!... LOOK!" And he noticed, that the crew were all knocked out. And Nia saw and wanted to take advantage, had quickly reacted. And she quickly elbowed Alex in the stomach, and ran to Feng. And Feng, immediately saw her brother reached from behind his waist, shouted," NO!" Now, Lloyd had seen the opportunity with Alex, and shot him twice in the chest. And Richie at the time, had got up from being knockout, and grabbed the knife again. And he quickly ran, and stabbed Feng in the back. And Feng caught off guard, in pain, had turned and kicked Richie. And the officer takes aim at Richie, shooting him five times as he falls dead. And he ran and helped Feng, as he staggered in pain. And the people watching from the bar begin to approach them. Now, Nia in concern for Feng, slowly shouted, "SOMEBODY HELP US!" And Lloyd had saw the men on the ground move, and aimed at them saying," Don't move!" And he seen a gun near Alex's body, and immediately called for an ambulance.

Chapter 11

And the ambulance shows up, along with two cop cars. And the paramedics had rushed to Feng, and the arrests were being made. Now, Lloyd then explained the situation with Nia to the officers, and his partner Hill. And the bar owner with the customers, stood away and watched everything. And when asked questions, the owner spoke up. Now, Lloyd then receives a text message from Lugo, as his partner watched. And Hill, noticing his arm was still stiff, had asked, "How's your arm?" And he slowly moving it, answered," I've had better days, bro." He's partner then laugh at the comment, and out of concern says, "Listen, don't try to be a hero next time, we're partners... Lewis will be here shortly." And he laughed at the remark walking away. And he begins to check the message from Lugo. And the text read, "We finally got Steve Liang. His crew, and the mob." And Lloyd smiled at the message and felt a sense of accomplishment.

And he seen Feng go inside the ambulance. And he met with him in the ambulance asking, "Why don't you become a cop, Feng?" And Feng had frowned answering, "Now is not a good time, Officer Llyod... I'm in pain." Now, Lloyd had glanced at a paramedic asking," Is it bad?" And the paramedic saw him sit, answered," It wasn't too deep." And the officer becoming sarcastic, had glanced at Nia near her brother body asked, "Feng, was she worth it?" And he being annoyed, answered, "You killed her brother, and had those thugs arrested... Why are you asking me?... And did you even say freeze?" And they look at each other, laughing on the way to the hospital. Now, Nia had glanced at the ambulance leaving, feeling sorry for him. And she began to shed tears, in remembrance of her brother. And the news reporter and crew, had just arrived. And 10 minutes later, the situation had made the news.

Now, these were the affairs that happened later. Feng had a good recovery, due to the knife not penetrating deep. And he, and Renee became good friends. And the Feng's had arrived back from Miami Florida. And their son then explained everything, that was on the news to them.

Michelle Feng within days, had reached out to the Feng's, wanting to perform in worship like Polly. And Polly agreed, and began to have one on one's with her at the Feng's residents. Now, Polly with the deacons at that time, had decided to have a tailormade priest robe for Lo. And the robe within days was made, and given to honor him. And he was amazed, and had appreciated the robe, seeing the crosses on the sleeves were in gold. And the robe colors, were black and red with golden trims. And there was a black cape, with a huge golden cross. And he at the time, kept having dreams of owning a church, and was shown the location. And he indeed, knew what the lord was saying to him.

Ken Feng at the time, was having thoughts on accepting Jesus into his life. And he wanted the joy, love and peace his brother's family had. So, he continued to watch, and study his brother's life. And he felt that Jesus may indeed, be the answer to all of this. And his daughter would invite him to church, but would always be given an excuse. But, she wouldn't give up. And she believed that her parents would eventually be saved, one day.

Mrs. Miles was kept in witness protection. And when she was asked to appear in court during the trial, she did it with a lawyer. And she told the Judge everything she knew. From her relationship with Shawn, to who he brought drugs from. And she, being a former member of Powers, had talked about them also. And when she was asked to identify Mr. Smith, she did.

And Ed, with a lawyer, had testified against Mr. Smith too. And he, was also placed under witness protection.

Detective Ronald and Mary had done their part appear in court also. Mary then made a comment to the judge about being happy. Happy, that this case didn't turn out to be a cold case. Now, Shawn's ex, had moved to New York City, to start her life over again.

Greg didn't have to face court due to Robbie's death. Even after, it was shown that he drew first.

Nia Yung, had moved back to New Jersey, shortly after to start a new life. And she indeed knew, that she and Feng were officially over.

And Angel continued seeing Amanda, and eventually got into a serious relationship.

Maggie Liang, had continued running the stores in peace. Seeing there was no heat or gang activities anymore. And the Garcia family, were appearing in court seated, to hear and know Steve's fate.

Officer Lloyd and Hill, were in court during the Steve Liang trail. And the court understood the self-defense for Feng and Nia, the civilians. And they were also present in court, and were ready to testify.

Vicky a week later, had left Lloyd for her ex. And she admitted, her true feelings to him, and had wanted to become friends instead.

Detective Lugo, Mary and Peter continued to uphold the law til this day. And they became a force to be reckoned with.

Wendy and her son had joined her sisters church, and accepted Jesus as their lord and savior. And she thanked her sister evanglist Judy green, for covering them in their time of need. And she later, gave her testimony.

Now, Larry and the rest of the mob, were each given 15 years for racketeering, and selling illegal firearms. And their lawyers did the best they could, but lost the fight. And Larry's gun shops, were immediately shut down. And this indeed made the news.

Mr. Lyor Smith was charged with drug trade. And he was sentenced to 30 years based on the evidence provided. And the crew were all sentenced differently, according to the crimes they had committed. Some were given 7 years, and others were given 11 years. Cowell was given 15 years being the muscle. And Lyor's lawyer, had spoken to the judge to have his time reduced but was declined.

Richie's mechanic shop, was shut down due to racketeering as well. And the strippers they slept with, didn't know much, but were tired of the abusiveness from the crew. And one stripper named Lori, in fear for her 16-year-old sister living with her, had spoken up. And the detectives were told that they're involvement was just shelter, sex and money. And the stripper also mentioned a meeting with Steve, that was supposed to happen.

Lisa, Robbie's girlfriend, saw Detective Mary while loading groceries. And when they conversed, she claimed not to know anything, due to their off and on relationship.

Roy and Mia had testified in court against Steve, and were kept in witness protection. Lucky and Chi were given 14 years for their rank, and keeping order in organized crime. And the rest of the crew were given 8 years. Charged by affiliation, with assault and battery told by the strippers. And this also included death threats to the gas station owners. And a tape was played by Terry earlier in court, regarding Chi's conversation with Lugo. And their lawyer tried to stop the tape from being played, but the judge wanted to hear it. And when the tape played, the lawyer recognizing his voice had felt embarrassed. Chi told about the 2 million from drugs, the mentioning of names and the gas operation. And he was embarrassed by the tape, and began to look down avoiding eye contact with Steve. Now, Steve seated next to Chi, gave him a stone-cold look, having thoughts of wanting him dead. And the Judge heard, and gazed at the jury in thought of this scheme being defraud.

And the two owners of the gas stations, with their lawyers, had later testified against the crew. And they were also kept in the witness protection.

And the Judge, by Lugo's help, had recognized that the new leader was indeed Steve including the untraceable phone and Lucky's gun. And the Judge knew then, that this would be the end to the evils in the city. Now, the judge then made known to Steve, that he and the mayor were cousins. And that he didn't like the misusing of the bible, for evil induct. And he, being a Christian, was a lover of the word. And when the judge asked him why the bible, he stood and answer," Because your honor, the world doesn't know the power it has!" And he knew he wasn't in the court's good graces at all. And he was now called forth, by a lawyer with a smirk. And after he was seated, and given the oath. He had denied many things, including an investor for anything. And his lawyer at the time, did the best he could to defend him, regardless of the evident's proven. And he later, was sentenced to 90 years to life. And the charges were organized crime, illegal firearms, assault and battery, defraud, tampering with evidence and first-degree Murder.

Now, three weeks later, he had accepted Jesus into his life by a saved inmate. No longer calling himself Lord, but Steve.

And the investor had moved on, cutting all ties with Steve. Seeing the plan had failed, due to Steve being captured. And the investor had felt that he could deny anything to do with him, until proven guilty.

Jasmine, with her lawyer, had cooperated with the agents to get a lesser sentence. However, she didn't know much about the investor. Jasmine, had mentioned to the agents in all seriousness, that Steve trusted no one. And the Garcia family, was happy that justice for Jane had happened.

Feng and Renee then had chemistry. And they sometime later, had decided to be in a relationship. And he, wanting his own place, had reached out to his uncle Ken, the realtor for a house. Two weeks later, with Ken and Lo's help, he got a house in the suburbs of New Haven, CT. And he worked for another club, becoming a lead bouncer for a short period of time. And she felt pressed, to introduce him to her father named Sylvester. And when the couple had spoken, a day later she called, and her father agreed to meet Feng. And she later, out of excitement, had reached out to Feng about the meet up. And her father, was always overprotective of her and her sister. And they all agreed to meet a week later, at a coffee shop, on a Tuesday at 2 p.m.

Now, it became Tuesday, and the time was 2 p.m. And Feng was the first one there, sitting close to the entrance, with few people around. And a waiter saw, and met with him asking," What can I get for you?" And he smiled saying," I'm waiting for my girlfriend, give me a minute." And the waiter had understood, and walked away. And he continues to wait patiently, looking out the window for De Ninos.

Now, Renee had arrived 15 minutes later, with Sylvester in his car, and parked across the street. And she turned the engine off, and was ready to meet up. And her father looks at the coffee shop asking," Where is he?... What's his name?" Now, Renee had saw Feng, and pointed him out saying," His name is Feng!... He's the big guy close to the entrance! "And he saw, and glanced at her saying, "Really!... I never seen this guy before... Where you meet him?" Renee answered, "Its a long story, pop." Now, Sylvester, now in thought of Lloyd, said," I still can't believe you haven't told me about this cop, Renee. "And she took a breather, answering," Ten minutes ago, I told you... Yeah, that guy wasn't important pop. I... Sylvester then cut her off saying," Cop or no cop, you should've told me. Renee... You and Monica is all I got... I'd like to know who you're seeing sometime, okay?" And Renee, avoiding an argument, had agreed by nodding yes. And she answers, "Okay... So, are you ready to meet my boyfriend, pop?" And he opened his door, and got out, closing it back. And she, receiving no answer, was left with the thought being okay, that went well. And she had opened, and quickly closed her door, as her father waited on her. And she saw that the road was clear, says," Pop, please don't scare him!" And he smirks at the remark, as they begun to cross answered," I gotta see what he's made of!"

And they came inside, and sat at the table across from Feng. And a waiter saw and came over asking," Are you all ready to order?" And she glanced at the fellas answering," Just three coffees... Two coffees regular, and one black with two sugars.... Thanks." And the waiter had written down the order and left. Now, Sylvester then asked," How are you?" Feng now focus on him answered, "I'm good." Sylvester says," I'm pretty sure you know I'm Renee's father... And I want what's best for her, understand with what's going on in this world... So, tell me a little bit about yourself." Renee then frowned, and said," Pop, I told you everything about him." And he nodded and said," Indeed you did." Feng knew he needed to say something, answers," Well, where do I start, right?... Born and raised around here. Christian background, and was a lead bouncer...." And Sylvester then interrupts asking, "Was?" Feng had seen the no nonsense look on his face, answered, "I'm going to college to become an IT worker... Information Technology." And Sylvester continued to stare at him, and tries to figure out his character. Renee watching, had said, "Daddy?" And Sylvester then asked," And your folks, they still married? And Feng, not being intimidated by him answers," Yes.... They've been together for a very long time... I'd like Renee to meet them one day." Now, Sylvester remembering what she had told him says," Renee had mentioned that your adopted... So, your folks....." Feng interrupted and answers," My father died in the line of duty, and my mother isn't in my life... She gave me to a loving family... Now, can I ask you a question?" Sylvester liking his forwardness, answered," Sure." And Feng out of curiosity asked," Your folks still married?"

And Renee watched her father look down deep in thought said," Daddy?" And he then focused back on Feng, answers," My mother stepped out on my father on my fourteenth birthday. My mother, and his best friend, had gotten caught at a room next to mines... She hugged me farewell, before I blew out my candles... And that was the last time I saw her. My father has always been there for me, Feng... I can't believe I shared that with you." And he, given it some thought says," So, our mothers abandon us... Now, are you what's best for my daughter?" Now, Feng reached for her hand in comfort, saying," I am... I can make her happy, sir... I forgave my mother, thanking her for giving me to a loving family... Have you forgiven your mother, sir?" And Sylvester not liking sir, says," Don't call me sir, but Sylvester.... Forgiveness, you said?" And the waiter came, and gave their coffees asking," Do you all need anything else?" Renee answered," Give us a minute." And the waiter then left.

Renee had glanced at her father again in thought said," Daddy?" And he smiled at her saying, "I like him, Feng's alright... Feng, I suppose you know what will happen if you break my little girl's heart, right? "He answered," I'm in it for the long haul, Sylvester." Sylvester, liking the comment now drunk, and finished his coffee says," Alright... Let's see what's on the menu. "Renee couldn't stop smiling, and had called for a waiter. Now, Sylvester, in thought of her sister asked," What's your sister doing?" She answers," Probably hanging out with Tommy Toretto again." And the waiter now came, and took everyone's order. And they had spent most of the afternoon, getting to know each other on a good note. And Sylvester indeed, had approved of Feng.

And that same afternoon, at the Yung's home in New Jersey. Nia was talking with her aunt Lilliana, in the living room, about the situation with the family. Lilliana was a very abusive and manipulative person. And some of the women in their family, were witches like herself, wanting control over anything. And she was introduced to witchcraft young, by her grandmother. And Lilliana says," So, Alex is dead. Steve is in jail, and your back... This man, thing." Nia with her arms cross interrupted, replied, Feng... Feng is his name." Lilliana, disappointed, shouts, "WHATEVER!... HAD YOU'D NOT BEEN WITH HIM; ALEX WOULD STILL BE ALIVE... STEVE NOT IN JAIL." And Nia arguably says," How could you say that!... The cops were watching Steve, and stupid Alex!!... Like, why am I even listening to you right now!" And Lilliana, had seen tears streaming down her cheeks said," I don't know about you, Nia... Maybe it was the sex, I don't know... Do you still love this man?" Nia looking down answers," I... I do." And a thought then hit Nia, and she asked ,"Question, why is it always my fault?... I had already told you, that the cops were watching them! "Now, Lilliana then frowned and slapped her. And she saw her shocking reaction, and with an attitude says," I blame you for Alex's death... You could have stopped him, Nia!... Was Feng involved with the cops?... Was he? Answer me!" Nia with her hand to the cheek, shouted," YES!... HIS FRIEND IS A COP!" Now, Lilliana with a no-nonsense look, begins to cross her arms. And she, in a calmly manner said," You knew this would happen!" And Nia then got on her knees, and cried wanting to hold her aunt shouts," NO! NO!... I LOVE MY FAMILY!" Now, Lilliana, moving away from her shouts," DON'T TOUCH ME!... I DON'T CARE WHAT ALEX DID, YOU PUT YOUR FAMILY FIRST! "Lilliana saw her trying to hold her again, shouted," WHAT DID I SAY!... DON'T TOUCH ME!!" And Nia nodded in agreeance, now looking down. And she knew then, she had a strong hold on Nia. And in a conning voice, said," Nia... How do we make this right, right?... I mean, why should Feng live, right? "Now, Nia then looks up confused asking," You want me to kill him? "And Lilliana asked," Why did you come back to me?... I took good care of you, and Alex is why, right?" Nia wiping her tears answers," You have, but you're asking me to kill him." Now, Lilliana becoming curious about the connection asked," Did Alex know about Feng?" Nia begins to cry again, answering," No! I... I... I would've told him.... He and Steve." Nia, in thought of everything, continues to cry. Now, Lilliana says," Revenge will make this right, Nia!... I want revenge for what Feng did to you brother." And she answered," It wasn't Feng that killed him... It was a cop." Now, Lilliana continues to mess with her head, saying," Admit it's your fault, Nia... This whole thing, you know how to make it right." And Nia nodded in agreeance. And she smirk and said, "Good girl."

Now, Lilliana's boyfriend named Kai, had opened and closed the door. And he saw and knew something had happened. Kai was a tough guy, with a wicked pass. And he knew what his girlfriend was into, but was under her lusting spell. And she, undermining his lost facial expression, had asked ," How was work?" And he, seeing a beautiful young woman on her knees wiping her tears, in a sarcasm manner answered," Fine... No... how was your day, right?... Who's this?" And she glanced at Nia saying ," She's my niece." And she then remembers he has a gun, so she asked," Hey!... Are you still license to carry?" And he then felt the question was awkward, but answered," I am, why?" She then walked over to him, and gently touched his face. And she in a sweet manner voice, says," My niece wants to learn how to uses a gun, to protect herself... I'm speaking up for her... I need you to teach her, please." And he thought on it, looking into her eyes out of lust. And she joined hands with him, leading him upstairs to their room. And Nia saw but remained on her knees, still in thought of everything. And as the evening came, she couldn't sleep.

And the next morning, Lilliana was seated at the kitchen table with Nia. And she had a plan to get revenge for Alex. But, her real plan, was to set Nia up for murder. So, she'd be out of her life for good. And she had provided and met her needs, to keep her focus. And she knew her niece was the curse breaker in the family, and didn't want her to deliver them. And she also removed Nia's star, meaning her destiny, performing witchcraft alone in her room. And the spirit she moved with, was a female falling angel, by the name of Lilith. And Lilith, being the mother of mermaid spirits dealt with sex. And she knew the deep things, like having children with demons through masturbation. And how to use demonic music, to link dimensions to traffic demons from another world, to this world and such. And she loved using the big mirror in her room, to talk to demons. And the demon that would come to visit her the most, was named Lielie. And the demon would come, to look, talk and act like her.

Nia at the time, was already oppressed. And she had wanted to prove her loyalty again to her aunt. Now, Lilliana, being unfamiliar with the Feng's, had one day asked about them. Nia answered, They're a saved Christian family, that loves Jesus. And she, hearing the name Jesus, wanted no parts of them. And she then asked about the officer who killed her brother. Nia then spoke about Feng's friendship with him, but knew very little. And Lilliana then felt, he wasn't a threat, says," This man has no covering at all... No blood of Jesus around him." And she smirked, and felt he'd be an easy prey. And she continued to go over the plan, again and again. And Nia was also told, if she failed to never come back again. And she, with confidence, refused to fail the family, but more her aunt. And she felt this would save and reconnect them.

Kai a few days later, began to teach Nia how to shoot at a gun range. And she, within a week, had learned it so fast, that it impressed him. And he, not knowing the truth, enjoyed her more than his own girlfriend. And he tried to get her to open up, but she wouldn't. Now, Lilliana, later with a charming bracelet, had come to her. And she asked her for permission to give, lying that it was for good luck. And Nia thought nothing of it, answered yes. And she wore it, and felt completely different. And she didn't know that it was cursed, and had kept her feeling revengeful. And Lilliana would always ask her customers or people in general for permission, and granted yes, was a gateway to curse anything.

Now, two days later, Nia had seen a strong vision in bed. And she saw two women, and six men standing before an altar, looking at a cross. And they kneeled, and began to worship. And she had recognized the two men and woman being Lo, Polly and Feng. And she then saw Lo get up, and faced her. And he in all seriousness, says," To close the portal, you need to put three crosses next to each other, on the mirror with anointing oil. And she wasn't aware of the mirror situation that he knew. And she waking up, understood the dream, knowing they're sold out to Jesus. And she had kept the vision to herself ignoring the message. And she glanced at the bracelet, on the dresser for comfort. And puts it back on, and was blinded by the affect.

And her aunt had kept her till August, feeling the time was right. And she at the time, wanted more power, and was waiting for a meeting with an underworld queen named Merna. And her boyfriend watched, and thought Nia's behavior was very strange. Now, Brenda and Katie would call her from time-to-time, but she already had distanced herself. And she wasn't herself, and had become numb and grew to be cold hearted. And when she was released, she got on a plane, with only the charm to New Haven, already convinced that revenge was the answer.

This story is aligned with Canaries story of forgiveness. I hope you all have been blessed by this book. Remember, Jesus is lord. And if you haven't received Jesus as your lord and savior, please go to Romans 10:9-10 and ask him. And look for the next book, God bless.

www.ingramcontent.com/pod-product-compliance
Lightning Source LLC
LaVergne TN
LVHW021716060526
838200LV00050B/2699